PSYCHOLOGY WORLDS ISSUE 33

CONNOR WHITELEY

Any questions about the book, rights licensing, or to contact the author, please email connorwhiteley@connorwhiteley.net

INTRODUCTION

I have to admit that September 2025 is very, very weird for me. Normally, in these September issues of the Psychology Worlds magazine, I talk about how I'm excited for the new academic year, I'm looking forward to learning so much more at university and I'm excited for the different social opportunities.

That isn't happening this year because I've finished my Masters and I need to get a job.

Do not get me wrong, I am still excited because whatever job I get, whatever topics I write psychology articles about and more will mean I get to learn a lot and have great social interactions. Yet I will not be at university where I have been for the past six years.

Therefore, in case you're like me, concerned about the uncertainty, finding a job and thriving after university. Then this month's issue of the Psychology Worlds magazine will be able to provide you with some great, fascinating and insightful psychology facts to offer you some escapism from the real world for a while.

Believe me, when hunting for jobs feels like a soul-sucking experience, you need some escapism and I am more than happy to provide.

We kick off this issue with one of my most popular psychology articles in *What Is Interpersonal Psychotherapy?* Personally, I was rather surprised when this article took off and became really popular, because I didn't realise how mainstream this form of psychotherapy was. Therefore, in this insightful article, you get to learn about what is interpersonal psychotherapy, how it works, who benefits from this therapy and more. If you enjoy learning about clinical psychology then this will be a great article for you.

In *What Therapists Should Tell Clients About Their First Therapy Session,* you get to learn about the different tips, techniques and information that therapists need to use in their first session with clients. I always say that going to therapy is really brave and requires a lot of courage because we are expecting clients to open up about their deepest, darkest secrets to us. We are effectively strangers.

This is why it's important to cover certain things with clients in a first session. Hence, the need for this fascinating article.

The third article in this issue is *Why Is Each Psychology Subfield An Echo Chamber*. I really enjoyed writing and reflecting on this fact and it provided me with a lot of food for thought after a rather shocking interaction with my friends at university. This is a must-read for sure.

Stepping away from mental health and clinical psychology entirely for our penultimate article, in *How Does Categorising Our Relationships Impact Morality.* Originally, I wrote this article for my book *Moral Psychology* and it really is a thought-provoking look at our relationships, morality and how we deem the ingroup as more moral than the outgroup. If you have an interest in morality, social psychology and intergroup relations then you need to read this great article.

Finally, we round off the article section of this issue with another form of psychological therapy in *What Is Acceptance and Commitment Therapy.* Also, on the theme of this issue, as part of my specialist rape counselling, I needed to do a lot of acceptance and commitment in my own life. I needed to accept that I couldn't get rid of my rape trauma and I needed to live with it and over time it has thankfully weakened its grip over my life.

More on that later on though.

All those fascinating articles come before the two full-length books in this issue. Firstly, *Suicide Psychology* makes a return to these pages and I have a very personal relationship with this book but you wouldn't know it. I wrote this book about suicide long before I was comfortable writing about my own personal experiences, so even though I have tried to end my life three times in 2024. This book was written before that and I didn't touch on my suicidal idealisation as a teenager.

However, *Suicide Psychology* provides you with a lot of truths, facts and figures so you can understand and fight against the damaging, toxic myths that allow suicide to thrive. Suicide will always thrive in the darkness but with the knowledge contained in this book, we can fight against it.

And ultimately, save lives.

Finally, my brand-new book *Healing As A Survivor* makes its debut in these pages. I am so excited to share this book with you because it was hard to write, it was hard to organise and it was hard to release into the world because this is such a personal book to me. Yet I know it contains a lot of valuable clinical psychology insights, tips and knowledge that everyone will benefit from.

Now we understand all the enthralling psychology content in this issue, let's turn over the page and start exploring some psychology worlds.

WHAT IS INTERPERSONAL PSYCHOTHERAPY?

Besides from Cognitive Behavioural Therapy, the other form of psychotherapy that I have heard tons about is interpersonal psychotherapy. Personally, from what I have actually learnt about the therapy during my lectures, I prefer CBT to Interpersonal, but now I want to learn more. Therefore, in this clinical psychology podcast episode, you'll learn what is interpersonal psychotherapy, how does it work amongst other fascinating topics. If you enjoy learning about psychotherapy, clinical psychology and mental health then this is a great episode for you.

What Is Interpersonal Psychotherapy?

Interpersonal Psychotherapy is a focused, time-limited and evidence-based form of psychological therapy that is specifically designed to treat mood disorders. For example, depression and bipolar disorder. Since the main goal of this therapy is to improve the quality of a client's social functioning as well as their interpersonal relationships because this helps to reduce their psychological distress.

In addition, Interpersonal Psychotherapy uses four main strategies to help a client resolve their mental health difficulties. Firstly, Interpersonal Psychotherapy helps a client to manage any unresolved grief they have. Secondly, Interpersonal Psychotherapy addresses any interpersonal deficit a client has, like their involvement in unfulfilling social relationships and social isolation. Thirdly, this therapy can be useful for helping a client deal with a tough life transition like a major move, divorce or retirement. Finally, Interpersonal Psychotherapy is generally recommended for clients dealing with interpersonal disputes that come from conflicting expectations. For example, the expectations from family members, partners, close friends as well as coworkers.

How Does Interpersonal Psychotherapy Work?

The therapy was developed over 20 years ago as a treatment option for Major Depression and in recent years, the therapy has gained popularity. Since therapists that use Interpersonal Psychotherapy believe that a change in a client's social environment is a key factor in the onset of depression as well as a maintaining factor.

Furthermore, whilst the therapy was originally designed for adults, it has been modified so it can be effectively used for elderly and adolescent clients too.

Also, the therapy first appeared in the literature as part of a study looking at the effectiveness of anti-depressants and it was found to be just as effective as medication.

Personally, I really like that Interpersonal Psychotherapy acknowledges the "triggering event" in all but name when it comes to depression. Since I know and fully acknowledge that the Diathesis-Stress model is not perfect at all, but I like the model because it's useful for explaining how a stressful life event can trigger depression. Interpersonal Psychotherapy takes that explanation to a practical level.

In addition, Interpersonal Psychotherapy doesn't really focus on past relationships or the past in general, compared to other psychodynamic approaches. Instead Interpersonal Psychotherapy draws on internal conflicts without making them the focus of the therapy. So there are some similarities between Interpersonal Psychotherapy and psychodynamic approaches but it is more of an off-shoot of that old approach rather than a sibling therapy.

Equally, Interpersonal Psychotherapy is different from Cognitive Behavioural Therapy and similar approaches because whilst Interpersonal Psychotherapy does focus and deal with maladaptive behaviours and thoughts, it only does this if the maladaptive behaviours and thoughts apply to interpersonal relationships.

As a result of Interpersonal Psychotherapy is trying to change the client's relationship patterns instead of the associated depressive symptoms and it targets the relationship difficulties that end up making these depressive symptoms more severe and common.

Overall, Interpersonal Psychotherapy is less directive than cognitive behavioural therapy because whilst the therapy focuses on the client's specific problem areas without focusing on their personality traits.

Personally, something I do like about Interpersonal Psychotherapy is that it takes the "best" pieces from two completely different approaches to mental health and it combines them rather seamlessly. Therefore, clients can benefit from the insights gained from the internal conflicts idea from psychodynamic approaches and the targeting of maladaptive behaviours and thoughts from cognitive behavioural approaches without having to pull along and deal with the other facets of the two approaches.

I like how this therapy knows it has to deal with interpersonal relationships and that is all it does. I almost admire that sort of focus.

What Can A Client Expect From Interpersonal Psychotherapy?

Similar to Cognitive Behavioural Therapy, Interpersonal Psychotherapy can be done as part of individual or group therapy sessions over 12 to 16 weeks. As well as this therapy makes use of homework, interviews and continuous assessment by the therapist being done over a number of phases.

Before I talk about the different phases, group and individual sessions of Interpersonal Psychotherapy work in similar ways. Since group sessions are semi-structured, time-limited and they focus on interpersonal dynamics. Whereas unlike the individual sessions, group therapy sessions offer clients more opportunities to practice their interpersonal skills in a safe and supportive environment. As well as group sessions typically include pre-, mid- and post-treatment meetings individually with the therapist to review the client's progress, goals and strategies.

I have to admit that I don't typically think too much about group session therapies, because I know they are useful but I haven't really seen them as extremely useful compared to individual sessions. Yet I think group sessions are brilliant for Interpersonal Psychotherapy because the entire point of this therapy is to improve social skills, and you really can't practice social skills to a large extent if it is only the client and the therapist. So it's really good that group therapy sessions are used a lot in Interpersonal Psychotherapy if a client wants it.

Moreover, the first phase of Interpersonal Psychotherapy typically involves one to three sessions where the therapist assesses the client's depressive symptoms, close relationships, social history as well as any changes in relationship expectations or patterns. Afterwards, the therapist works with the client to implement a treatment plan specific to any "problem" areas that they've identified with the client.

Then over time as the treatment continues and progresses, the targeted problem area will hopefully change.

Furthermore, it's good to be aware here that like most other psychotherapies, Interpersonal Psychotherapy changes as a client goes through it. Since a therapist's recommended strategies might change as the client's problem area improves.

When Is Interpersonal Psychotherapy Used?

As I mentioned earlier, Interpersonal Psychotherapy was originally developed as a treatment for depression but in the past few decades, it is being effectively used to treat a wide range of other mental health conditions. For example, drug and alcohol addiction, eating disorders, bipolar disorder, dysthymia, perinatal depression as well as other mood disorders.

Clinical Psychology Conclusion

At the end of this slightly shorter podcast

episode, I have to admit that I am really glad that we've learnt about Interpersonal Psychotherapy because it is a very useful and interesting therapy targeting interpersonal skills and social functioning. And if a client has a mental health condition that is being maintained or caused by a lack of "good" interpersonal skills then this could be a great option for them.

And I am still really pleased that it draws on different approaches to mental health, because I fully believe that no one approach holds all the answers and it is only by combining the best pieces of different approaches that we'll be able to help our clients to the best of our abilities amongst the other attributes that makes an effective therapist but you get my point. Never think you need to be boxed into only using a single approach or therapy, because part the fun of psychotherapy is there are always more interesting, exciting, fascinating concepts and techniques to learn.

Clinical Psychology References and Recommended Reading

Cuijpers, P., Donker, T., Weissman, M. M., Ravitz, P., & Cristea, I. A. (2016). Interpersonal psychotherapy for mental health problems: a comprehensive meta-analysis. *American Journal of Psychiatry*, *173*(7), 680-687.

Heisel, M. J., Talbot, N. L., King, D. A., Tu, X. M., & Duberstein, P. R. (2015). Adapting interpersonal psychotherapy for older adults at risk for suicide. *The American Journal of Geriatric Psychiatry*, *23*(1), 87-98.

Huibers, M. J., Cohen, Z. D., Lemmens, L. H., Arntz, A., Peeters, F. P., Cuijpers, P., & DeRubeis, R. J. (2015). Predicting optimal outcomes in cognitive therapy or interpersonal psychotherapy for depressed individuals using the personalized advantage index approach. *PloS one*, *10*(11), e0140771.

Klerman, G. L., & Weissman, M. M. (1994). Interpersonal psychotherapy of depression: A brief, focused, specific strategy. Jason Aronson, Incorporated.

Lemmens, L. H. J. M., Arntz, A., Peeters, F. P. M. L., Hollon, S. D., Roefs, A., & Huibers, M. J. H. (2015). Clinical effectiveness of cognitive therapy v. interpersonal psychotherapy for depression: results of a randomized controlled trial. *Psychological Medicine*, *45*(10), 2095-2110.

Lemmens, L. H., Galindo-Garre, F., Arntz, A., Peeters, F., Hollon, S. D., DeRubeis, R. J., & Huibers, M. J. (2017). Exploring mechanisms of change in cognitive therapy and interpersonal psychotherapy for adult depression. *Behaviour research and therapy*, *94*, 81-92.

Markowitz, J. C., Petkova, E., Neria, Y., Van Meter, P. E., Zhao, Y., Hembree, E., ... & Marshall, R. D. (2015). Is exposure necessary? A randomized clinical trial of interpersonal psychotherapy for PTSD. *American Journal of Psychiatry*, *172*(5), 430-440.

Sockol, L. E. (2018). A systematic review and meta-analysis of interpersonal psychotherapy for perinatal women. *Journal of affective disorders*, *232*, 316-328.

Weissman, M. M., Markowitz, J. C., & Klerman, G. L. (2017). *The guide to interpersonal psychotherapy: updated and expanded edition*. Oxford University Press.

Wilfley, Denise E., & Shore, Allison L. (2015). Interpersonal Psychotherapy. In International Encyclopedia of the Social & Behavioral Sciences (pp. 631-636).

Wurm, C, Robertson, M, & Rushton, P. (2008). Interpersonal psychotherapy: An overview. Psychotherapy in Australia, 14(3), 46-54.

BESTSELLING AUTHOR OF FORENSIC PSYCHOLOGY
CONNOR WHITELEY
HOW TO IMPROVE YOUR RELATIONSHIPS
A SOCIAL PSYCHOLOGY, DEVELOPMENTAL PSYCHOLOGY AND ATTACHMENT THEORY GUIDE TO RELATIONSHIPS

WHAT SHOULD THERAPISTS TELL CLIENTS ABOUT THEIR FIRST SESSION?

When a client comes to a therapist and books a first session, the client will be anxious, concerned and they will have a lot of questions. This is perfectly normal but therapists might want to take the time to tell clients a few pieces of information to help them understand what's going to happen amongst other things. These answers will help the client to relax and not be as stressed about their first therapy session. Something that will hopefully change their lives for the better. Therefore, in this clinical psychology podcast episode, we're going to explore the questions clients have for therapists about their first session and how therapists might want to answer these questions. If you enjoy learning about clinical psychology, psychotherapy and mental health, then you'll like today's episode for sure.

Note: as always nothing on this podcast is ever any sort of medical, legal or official advice.

What Therapists Should Tell Clients About Their First Therapy Session?

Also, I want to note here that whilst this podcast episode is more aimed at private therapists and mental health professionals because I presume it is easier for these therapists to contact their clients. I think this is still a useful podcast episode for public sector workers because you can learn and understand our clients more. As well as you might want to adopt answering some of these questions into your own service, just a thought.

Do Therapists Offer Free Introduction Sessions?

A lot of clients who have never been to therapy before and aren't 100% sure about its value can be concerned about the cost, so a lot of clients like the idea of having a free session before they commit to spending money.

A lot of therapists do offer free sessions in one form or another. For example, most therapists offer free phone consultations or shorter free sessions, like my therapist offers a free 20-minute in-person session. These free sessions are useful for seeing if a therapist is the right fit for you, because there is a chance that finding a therapist that is right for you is a process of trial and error.

However, I want to stress that different therapists often debate the ethics and the finances of offering free sessions, because they have to pay the bills, earn a living and they went to university or did a Level 4 course to get their qualifications. Don't they have the right to be paid for their time, skill and work?

Therefore, whenever a therapist talks with a potential future client, it is useful to talk about any free sessions they offer. For example, I know my therapist is willing to talk to people about an alternative payment plan if they're on a lower income.

Will Therapists Ask About Family History?

I think because I study clinical psychology, this isn't a question that pops up for too much because I always knew the answer was yes. But some clients will not know this and they will be a little concerned about sharing aspects of their family to someone who is effectively a stranger to them.

As a result, it's useful to share with potential clients that family history will be spoken about (the vast majority of therapists do ask about it) at some point in the course of therapy. Since it's important to learn about any family history of depression, anxiety, addiction or any other mental health problems.

Although, it is worth noting not every therapist likes getting this information in the first session and this largely depends on their personal preference or theoretical orientation. Which I understand because some people might want to wait a session or two before getting this deeply personal and potentially very sensitive and triggering information from a client.

Is It Okay For Clients To Cry In Therapy?

I was actually rather some people didn't think it was okay to cry during therapy, because to me, therapy is a deeply emotional process that will bring up emotions, traumatic experiences and more. I think I've even come close to crying two or three times in my therapy sessions, so it's strange that people don't think crying is okay in therapy.

Granted, I know at least in the UK, there is a lot of societal and gender social norms at play here. Like, the absolute rubbish idea that men shouldn't cry amongst other myths, so it is just annoying that these rubbish ideas continue into the therapy room.

Somewhere that is meant to be a safe space.

Overall, it is perfectly okay to cry in therapy because the therapist will respond in an empathetic and non-judgemental way. And if crying embarrasses your client or a client wants to cry but they can't because of an emotional block, then this might be something to explore with them in therapy.

Is It Normal To Be Nervous Starting Therapy?

Personally, I would find it really strange if someone wasn't nervous about starting therapy, because I've studied psychology for half a decade now at university level (that is thought) and I know a lot about therapy. Yet I was still really nervous because as I always say, when it comes to therapy, we are asking clients to reveal their deepest, perhaps darkest secrets, thoughts and behaviours. Something that our clients might be ashamed of, and we are asking them to tell us all of these things to us even though we are effectively strangers.

That takes an immense amount of courage but it is extremely scary too.

Thankfully, we might want to tell our clients that as they get to know us, this nervousness starts to decrease and if a client still feels anxious about the therapy after a few sessions, then the client should probably talk about this with us.

I remember from my first and second lot of therapy. I was really nervous about my first lot of therapy because I had never done it before, I didn't know what was going to happen and I wasn't sure if this was the right thing to do. Then I was a little nervous about my second lot of therapy with a different one at the university, but both went fine and I really liked them both.

Should A Client Prepare For Their First Therapy Session?

In my experience, this really depends on the individual client because some people are happy to just go into therapy without a plan or doing any pre-work at all. Whereas I know other clients like to think about topics they want to discuss and more. As well as clients like to think about the information they really, really want the therapist to know in their first session.

Equally, therapists don't really care if a client does prep work beforehand or not, so it might be an idea to tell a client that prep work isn't needed. Unless the client finds it helpful themselves.

Personally, I remember when I went for my first lot of private therapy, I wrote down the following to help me prepare for my first session.

"Tell Her About

- General family structure
- My self-harm and suicide stuff
- Beating threats, invalidation
- Coming out- X for 2 weeks and invalidation and the "conditions" (I had to live under)
- Last week
- Guilt I feel now

What Do I Want Out of This?

- Healthier, more adaptive coping mechanisms for dealing with negative emotions
- Self-acceptance
- Less guilt
- Dealing with the lies

Protective factors

- Podcast audience and readers
- My close friends

- Wanting to come to therapy
- Me wanting an ASC diagnosis and going to continue support at university."

Therefore, as you can see, to help me feel prepared and ready for my first therapy session I did a little bit of prep work and I thought about what I wanted to tell her. I also did a similar thing for my bunch of therapy at the university, so I wrote down the following:

"Areas Of Concern

Who am I?- feel lost now

Don't care about degree, just doing it and unsure about future now I'll live

Fragility and lack of resilience nowadays

Also, I want to do some work on friends and perceptions. Am I expecting too much of friendships?"

Now I have to admit it was fascinating looking at these notes because they are really good snapshots of what I was thinking and feeling in certain parts of my life. Even though they were only a few months ago to be honest, so it's interesting and it's great to see how far I've come.

Overall, I hope these short little examples have shown you and helped you to understand how some clients might want to prepare for their first session. Even though I never actually used these notes in my first sessions, but I found them useful to do at the time.

What Does A Therapist Ask In A First Session?

I was no different from any other client when I went for my first session. I had no idea what to expect, no idea what was going to be asked and it was difficult. This is why this podcast episode is rather useful for psychology students because this helps us to understand what actually happens in a first therapy session as well.

Therefore, it might be useful for clients to know that first therapy sessions are typically board brushstrokes about what has brought them to therapy, their general autobiography and then towards the end of the session, the therapist and client talk about what the rest of the sessions should cover.

In addition, therapists should tell clients, they will probably ask about the specific mental health difficulty that has made them want to come to therapy, what the client wants to achieve from therapy, any therapeutic experiences the client has had in the past and a brief life story.

Also, in the first session at the beginning, you'll do some basic paperwork with the client for obvious reasons. For instance, my therapist got me to complete and sign a counselling contract, some medical information and she explained to me her therapeutic orientation, which I learnt a lot from and I have discussed on previous podcast episodes.

Clinical Psychology Conclusion

When it comes to psychotherapy, I will always advocate for empirically-supported therapies because they can be brilliant, useful and they can change someone's life for the better. I am proof of that and my life is a million times better than it was before therapy.

However, this improvement doesn't mean my first therapy session was easy. I was still nervous, concerned and I had no idea what to expect, so with this podcast focusing on psychology students and psychology professionals, I hope you now have a better understanding of how our clients might feel before they start therapy. You might want to use this information to help reassure them before their first session or not, that's okay but you have the understanding and the knowledge and that can be a powerful thing.

Especially, when it comes to improving someone's life by decreasing their psychological distress, giving them hope and helping them change their life for the better.

Clinical Psychology Reference

https://www.psychologytoday.com/gb/basics/therapy/your-first-therapy-session

WHY IS EACH PSYCHOLOGY SUBFIELD AN ECHO CHAMBER?

I absolutely have to admit that it was really difficult to pick just one reflection to share from my brand-new book *Clinical Psychology Reflections Volume 4*. Since there are a lot of really interesting, thought-provoking and fascinating reflections on clinical psychology and psychology as a whole. Therefore, in this podcast episode, you're going to be learn about how different areas of psychology can be echo chambers at times, why this is a bad thing and how this could change. If you enjoy reflective practice, clinical psychology and psychology as a discipline, then you'll enjoy today's episode for sure.

<u>Extract From Clinical Psychology Reflections Volume 4 (COPYRIGHT 2024 Connor Whiteley)</u>

I should probably say up front that the applied psychology subfields, like forensic psychology, clinical psychology and developmental psychology, are probably the exceptions to this rule, but I want to explore my point first of all. And I want to mention the limits and drawbacks of this question about clinical psychology at the end.

I'll start off by explaining this generally before I explain the flat out weird inspiration that kicked off the idea behind this reflection.

If we take a step outside clinical psychology for a moment and look at the three "main" approaches to behaviour. We have biological, cognitive and social psychology and all of these are fairly divorced from the others and this is great, but bad at the same time.

For example, it is brilliant that biological psychology only looks at our biology and how these processes impact our behaviour. It gives biological psychology researchers the freedom to explore our biology without getting mixed up with cognitive and social psychology.

The same goes for cognitive psychology. It's great that cognitive researchers can investigate our mental health and occasionally tap into biological or neuropsychology without worrying about social psychology variables.

Equally, it is so freeing that social psychologists can focus on how social situations and factors impact our own individual and group behaviour without having messy biological or cognitive factors interfering with the social behaviour.

And yes I know there is some overlap between these three disciplines as seen in social cognition, brain wave activity and how that impacts learning (what I did my dissertation on) and there are a handful of other crossovers too.

Yet my point is still hopefully clear. Each subfield of psychology is fairly or basically exclusively divorced from each other, which has its benefits and drawbacks.

In addition, the entire reason why this reflection is being written in the first place is because of a weird comment a friend of mine said. Now as psychology students we're all used to weird comments, but this comment I found really weird and mind-bending.

"That's cognitive psychology. I don't know if you clinical people are into that,"

Now I completely forget what we were talking about but I remember we were standing in the computer rooms where we were all testing our participants that day and when she said that I was shocked for a few easy reasons I will show you below (just bear in bear that psychological, cognitive and mental processes are the exact same thing)

- Psychotherapy
- Clinical psychologist
- Psychological therapy
- Cognitive Behavioural Therapy

Those four aspects are absolutely core features of clinical psychology and without those four, our profession could not function but this friend of mine actually believed clinical psychology was NOT interested in mental processes.

Personally, because this friend is great and I really like her, I'm going to be a little kinder than I normally would because this opinion makes no sense to me.

Yes, my friend is a cognitive person by trade and she is obsessed with cognitive psychology but again, she wants to work in clinical psychology. As well as this builds on perfectly from the last reflection, I really want people who want to work in clinical psychology settings to actually understand clinical psychology early on.

Since if she did take any clinical psychology modules or did any sort of clinical research then she would know without a shadow of a doubt that clinical psychology is all about the biological, psychological (cognitive) and social factors that interact together to develop and maintain a mental health condition.

Therefore, the fact that she thought clinical psychology couldn't give a rat's behind about cognitive processes, really hammered home to me just how isolated the theoretical and applied disciplines are.

And this I think is a massive shame because one of the biggest problems in the clinical psychology literature is that it is written by research academics in a way that either isn't understandable or usable by clinical practitioners. Basically making the research next to useless.

This is a problem that might start to be fixed in the future because I know there are clinical psychologists conducting research and lecturing at universities more than ever (apparently), but it is still a problem that needs to be overcome.

Also, if this problem starts with academics and people in the biological, cognitive and social psychology approaches themselves. Then in an ideal world, they would at least be given clinical psychology teaching or something by a real clinical psychologist so they could understand the practical sides of everything.

Since so much of clinical psychology is about practicalities and, at least in the UK, knowing what you can and cannot do in the NHS. This isn't a dig at anyone, it is just my opinions on the whole mess we find ourselves in.

Furthermore, what I really think this is about is communication and cooperation between the disciplines. I am not saying that the theoretical approach shouldn't do applied research or research that might be able to be adapted into something useful and practical because that is stupid. As well as everyone in academia should have the freedom to research whatever they want if it is legal, useful and ethical.

However, what I am saying is that if we ever want researchers and students and academia as a whole to truly understand the applied disciplines and what clinical psychology actually cares about. There has to be more communication and cooperation across the disciplines and then that would have other benefits as well.

Especially since a clinical psychologist would bring the real-world experience and clinical expertise to a project, and an academic would bring the hard science methodology that clinical psychologists might not have done for years.

There is plenty of room for both if academia allows it to.

The age of echo chambers needs to end and the age of academia afterwards needs to be more useful to applied disciplines, cooperative and have a lot more communication for sure because clinical psychology cares about everything that would help them to decrease the psychological distress of their clients and improve lives.

That is all we care about at the end of the day.

Clinical Psychology Reference

Whiteley, C. (2024) Clinical Psychology Reflections Volume 4: Thoughts On Clinical Psychology, Mental Health and Psychotherapy. CGD Publishing. England

HOW DOES CATEGORISING SOCIAL RELATIONSHIPS IMPACT MORALITY?

Recently, I've been focusing a lot more on the psychology behind morality and what makes humans do "right" and "wrong" behaviours. A part of our morality is how we divide people up into different categories based on our relationship to them. This is a fascinating area of social psychology that I highly recommend you listen to today because you'll definitely learn a lot and you'll be thinking for sure. Therefore, in this social psychology podcast episode, you'll see the four types of different relationships people have, what these relationships involve and most importantly, how do these relationships impact moral dilemmas. If you enjoy learning about social relationships, decision-making and morality then you'll love today's episode.

How Could Relationships Impact Morality?

Now, I'll fully admit when I came across this research I wasn't entirely convinced that different types of relationships might impact different moral behaviours. Then I started thinking about it and I realised just how common this is. For example, two easy examples are, when I go out with a university friend of mine for dinner and it's the two of us, we both pay for our own dinners. That's what happens whenever I go out with friends to be honest. Yet I am willing to pay for the dinner of my closest friends because I'm closer to them and they're great. Whereas, if I'm having lunch with my friend that is also my supervisor (or will be in the future) at my University's Parkinson's centre, I have absolutely no ethical problems with letting him pay for my lunch. He has the job and I help him out a lot so it is sort of only fair.

In that example, you can see three different examples of relationships and how I approach the very common idea of paying for a meal differently.

Are these really moral behaviours?

If you had asked me before this podcast episode, I would have said these basic examples have nothing to do with morality, but some researchers disagree. Especially because morality is all about what behaviours are right and wrong in a given situation. I'm sure some of you would say I shouldn't want my supervisor to always pay (granted we don't go out for lunch that often and I do not abuse that kind offer), but some of you would agree.

Then when we start thinking about additional factors, this gets more complex. For example, what if my friend is poor and struggles with money? Should I automatically pay for their dinners to help them out? Or what if I was struggling with money for a time? Is it morally right for me to ask my friend to pay me dinner so I could eat that night?

Some of you would say yes, others would say that was an immoral favour to ask.

That's why this is a great topic to look at.

What Are The Four Types of Relationships And How Do These Impact Morality?

Looking at the work of anthropologist Alan Fiske (1991), he categorises human relationships into four different types.

Firstly, you have communal sharing relationships where our ingroups are basically the same as us in relevant ways. Some examples of this would include teams at work, military units as well as our family.

Secondly, you have equality matching. These are relationships where we view others as our equals. Like, people who we take turns with at home or work, or people we take care to maintain our impartiality with. I know this one is a little complicated, but don't worry, I'll explain these categories in more detail in a moment.

Thirdly, you have authority ranking where we rank ourselves and others in a hierarchy or to a position. For instance, caste, work titles or seniority.

Finally, you have market pricing where we view others as a trade partner. These are people we view through a contractual lens. For example, people who we interact with because they help us because we help them and vice versa.

As a result of these categories, Rai and Fiske (2011) argue humans are motivated to behave differently toward each of these categories. And one example of this is we're happy to share resources with our family members but we get annoyed when a friend keeps asking us for stuff without a thank you, them spending time to cultivate our friendship and without reciprocating the favour.

Now, let's explore these in more depth.

Communal Sharing and Morality

When it comes to communal sharing relationships, these focus on an attitude of unity towards the ingroup. Since as we all know, maintaining any ingroup is not easy at times and there will be problems. Therefore, there is high motivation to maintain the ingroup because the people in the ingroup want to benefit the group over and beyond people outside the ingroup.

Due to ingroup members believe they have a common fate, which they want to be positive. Therefore, maintaining communal relationships relies on tribalism and in a sense keeping the tribe "pure". Resulting in ingroup members being morally motivated to eliminate these threats, even if they come at a very high moral price.

Interestingly, an international example of this communal sharing that Rai and Fiske (2011) mention is the Hutu Ten Commandments that mention how the unity as well as the fate of the Hutu people are perceived to be threatened by the Tutsi. Resulting in this fuelling propaganda that led to the Rwandan genocide.

A more personal example would be family attitudes towards kicking out LGBT+ members of the family. I know from personal experience and stories with friends how family units want to remain united and pure so there is minimal conflict that leads to family breakdown. So sometimes the easiest option is just to kick out the queer member of the family, making them homeless and completely cut off from the family.

Notice how I never said the easy option is the moral option?

It's disgusting but some families are just immoral.

Equality Matching and Morality

Our next type of relationship is focused on striking equal balances, which leads to a lot of positive ideas about morality. For example, human rights are thankfully all about treating other people as equals, governments should always treat people with dignity and respect, as well as we should treat others how we want to be treated.

In addition, striking an equal balance helps humans to cooperate in situations where we can't distribute resources equally or when it comes to taking turns.

Originally, we evolved these rules to limit free-riders because no one likes them at all. So this led to humanity developing some very elegant cooperation norms, like tit-for-tat so we can all generally trust each other in our economic and social interactions.

These norms generally work because people are motivated to maintain these rules and equality, because acting immorally or against these rules, results in punishment.

I always like reading anthropology research from time to time because you get to learn about random tribes. Hence, the Hammurabi's code reflects the extreme lengths people can go to protect this balance, as does the ancient Babylonia ideal of an eye for an eye. Even today, there are many countries that continue to institutionalise balance-keeping by the process of capital punishment. A life for a life.

We could have an entire moral debate about the concept of "a life for a life" but I've already had that debate with some 15-year-old children this week, so I'm good and we generally understand how capital punishment and balance-keeping informs morality.

Authority Ranking And Moral Judgements

Whereas in these social relationships, people are motivated to maintain a hierarchy regardless of its type. This involves people respecting and deferring to an authority figure and this authority figure should provide protection and take responsibility to some extent for the subordinates' actions.

The easiest example of this is the military as well as military command structure and units.

Normally, this hierarchy and social relationship is beneficial for everyone involved. Since if we take a parental example, then a parent can demand respect from their young and vulnerable children. In exchange, the parent not only protects their children from harm but the parent comes to the child's defence too.

As you can see, it's useful for encouraging moral behaviour.

Unfortunately, this social relationship can cause immoral behaviour as well. For instance, people in leadership positions are often thought to be more entitled to the group's resources than other people. Like, CEOs having bigger offices, extra benefits and larger paychecks. I won't even get into that argument about whether this is moral or not. I think it depends.

Anyway, leaders can become corrupt and authoritarian too. Then if we remember Milgram's experiments, we realise subordinates are willing to follow extreme orders from authority figures even if it harms other people.

That is definitely not moral behaviour.

Market Pricing Impacting Moral Judgements

Our final type of social relationship comes from Market Pricing and these relationships are maintained by an in-between system of value to compare different goods. I get that was a weird explanation but what it means is this relationship is essentially an economic market where the people in these relationships are motivated to maintain proportionality.

In other words, make sure each other is providing equal value.

These economic principles can extend to the social world too, because when good and evil behaviours are weighed against each other, this is what people use to determine the best course of action.

If we look at the criminal justice system, juries have to decide how much time a criminal should spend in prison in relation to the seriousness of the crime, we expect a system of meritocracy at work where the promotion or pay rise goes to the most deserving employee, and commanders are meant to determine how many lost lives are worth an action for the greater good.

How Do These Categories Mix and Conclusion

It's hard to think of any social relationships that are only one of these four types of relationships because there is a lot of overlap. For instance, if we think about dividing up a bill after a nice dinner, this is hard because going out with friends could be Equality Matching (because we want equal friendships) and it could be Communal Sharing to be honest. Or if you're out for dinner with a supervisor/ friend, it could be Authority Ranking, Equality Matching and Marketing Pricing.

On the whole, the entire point of today's episode is to show you that moral outrage as well as feelings get hurt because of these different types of relationships. Especially when they don't match your expectations.

For example, I know a lot of great trans people and a part of medical transitioning are different surgeries if they want them. Therefore, if a friend of mine had a surgery with a six-week recovery time and I helped them out for the majority of that time. And I would feel really good because I helped out my friend and I did the right moral thing in this situation. Then I would be working on the assumption, this was a communal Sharing relationship because they're part of my ingroup and the common fate of the friendship group is tied together.

Then let's say if I later received an email and a bank transfer from my friend repaying me for my time and the email contained a list of the amount they were paying me for each thing I did for them.

This would be deeply hurtful because this friend would be categorising our friendship as a Market Pricing relationship instead of what I believed it to be.

Of course, this example has and will never happen, but similar hurt feelings have happened before to me. And this example is a good one showing how we categorise relationships impact our moral judgements. Because I'll tell you now I would never go above and beyond for a Market Pricing relationship in comparison to Communal Sharing relationship.

And this is a great little thinking exercise because we all have examples of these four relationships in our lives, so ask yourself this simple question:

How far would your moral behaviour go for the people in each type of relationship? Because there's a big difference between paying for a cheap dinner and being close enough to someone to want to spend six weeks with them after an operation.

What do you think?

Clinical Psychology References

Fiske, A. P. (1991). *Structures of social life: The four elementary forms of human relations: Communal sharing, authority ranking, equality matching, market pricing*. Free Press.

Fiske, A. P., Kitayama, S., Markus, H. R., & Nisbett, R. E. (1998). The cultural matrix of social psychology. In D. T. Gilbert, S. T. Fiske, & G. Lindzey (Eds.), *The handbook of social psychology* (4th ed., pp. 915–981). McGraw-Hill.

Rai, T. S., & Fiske, A. P. (2011). Moral psychology is relationship regulation: moral motives for unity, hierarchy, equality, and proportionality. *Psychological review*, *118*(1), 57.

Whiteley, C. (2022) Psychology of Relationships: The Social Psychology of Friendships, Romantic Relationships and More. CGD Publishing. England.

WHAT IS ACCEPTANCE AND COMMITMENT THERAPY?

After something personal happened last night, all I can think about today is trauma and considering this psychology podcast episode is already likely to be late going out, I didn't want to argue with myself. I just wanted to do an episode on something I was already thinking about because what we experience in our childhood can have a massive impact on our relationships. For example, what *we* think a healthy relationship and boundaries look like and how we believe the social world works. Therefore, in this clinical psychology podcast episode, you'll learn about how childhood trauma impacts relationships, how trauma survivors can improve their relationship boundaries and a lot more useful and insightful information. If you enjoy learning about mental health, trauma outcomes and a bit of social psychology then this is a great episode for you.

How Does Trauma Impact Relationships?

Not a single one of us is born with an innate understanding of healthy boundaries. We learn what boundaries are healthy and what isn't healthy in a relationship by trying out different things, learning about social relationships and unfortunately, getting hurt along the way. All of us go through life thinking we know what healthy boundaries are until one day or one moment, we realise what we thought was a healthy boundary actually isn't. For example, you might have a fight with your best friend and it doesn't go the way you expected and you or your friend is hurt. Equally, you might find relationships really overwhelming and other people might believe that you're simply too "sensitive". Finally, and this happens to me somewhat often, you find out that you aren't actually as close to someone as you thought and you start to feel like an outsider.

Personally, I'll be the first to say that I find interpersonal relationships quite overwhelming at times because of my disorganised attachment style that I'm working on. As well as having childhood trauma and autism makes it difficult to do the entire social relationship part anyway, especially with neurotypical people who don't exactly have the same communication style as me. I have no problem talking with anyone and I love forming those relationships, but honestly, it is hard for me to form deep and meaningful friendships and relationships.

Boundaries are sometimes a major problem for me because I don't understand them. Also, I didn't really have great role models in my life to model these behaviours from.

On the whole, we all learn in the end that boundaries are a fine balance between feeling safe and vulnerable in a relationship where we can share our authentic emotions whilst asserting our personal limits and needs with other people when we feel we need their support.

However, when childhood trauma is added into the mix, this adds additional layers of complexity into trying to understand what healthy boundaries in relationships are, because of their traumatic experiences.

How Does Childhood Trauma Affect Relationship Boundaries?

Unlike when adults experience trauma and their perception of healthy boundaries aren't always affected, children who experience trauma are different. Since children living in dangerous, neglectful or abusive situations nearly always have their sense of boundaries negatively impacted because they have to depend on untrustworthy adults just to survive. These children don't have any choice and as part of this survival process, a child's brain has to do some very intense work. Especially as, Jannia Fisher (a trauma specialist) explains in her book Healing The Fragmented Selves of Trauma Survivors:

"When attachment figures are abusive, the child's only source of safety and protection becomes simultaneously the source of immediate danger, leaving the child caught between two conflicting sets of instincts. On the one hand, they are driven by the attachment instinct to seek proximity, comfort, and protection from attachment figures. On the other hand, they are driven by equally strong animal defense instincts to freeze, fight, flee or submit…before they get too close to the frightening parent." (Fisher, 2017 p. 24)

In other words, as much as a child knows their caregiver is abusive or being neglectful, the child still wants to form an attachment and bond with them because the child innately knows they need the adult in order to survive.

Yet as the child tries to do this more and more, they experience a powerful and (I would say) almost horrific stress reaction that signals to their nervous system that a threat to their very survival is incoming so their body gets into fight-or-flight mode constantly.

To the child this means they learn very quickly that relationships are helpful because they are key to survival, but relationships are dangerous too. Therefore, the child adapts their perception of boundaries to fit this really weird paradox.

At the moment, I'm doing a lot of research and writing regarding attachment styles so this is really clear and tragic to read about in a trauma context.

Personally, I would love to say that this is wrong but it isn't. Based on my own experiences of having a very homophobic social environment and a lot of other things going on in other social situations. It's hard. You don't know what's safe, who to trust and you are always on edge just waiting for something bad to happen. It's horrible and over time, you can convince yourself that it is simply safer to be alone because if you don't let anyone in then no one can hurt you anymore.

Of course, your life gets really alone, isolated and awful if you continue that pattern of behaviour for too long.

In addition, I know we've never looked at Schema Therapy on the podcast before but within this form of psychotherapy, there are "mistrust/ abuse schemas" which can leave a person with more tolerance for being mistreated and have weaker boundaries. All because the person doesn't know any different. Making it quite the powerful revelation when the person realises that healthier boundaries are actually possible.

As a result, when a child makes a connection between their abuse or neglect that causes a traumatic stress response from their brain, so they either fight, flight, freeze or attach or feign with their attachment style or sense of boundaries. This leads to five different effects on the child's boundary style and as an aspiring or qualified psychologist it's important to understand these boundary styles so our approach to mental health work can be more trauma informed. Ultimately, helping us to support our clients feel safer and more in control in their relationships.

What Are The Five Boundary Styles?

As I mentioned in the last section, our mind and body have five reactions to trauma that impact how we perceive healthy relationship patterns. For example, firstly, there is the "fight" reaction where we believe we need to push our needs onto others, impose our own version of events or even attack other people if we think that it's necessary to preserve our urgent needs. This can lead to someone becoming self-absorbed in a relationship.

Secondly, you could react with a "flight" response where your childhood trauma has caused you to have anxiety around closeness and intimacy where you always find reasons to avoid getting too close or directly expressing an emotional need. This can lead to social and emotional isolation.

In my opinion, this second point definitely fits me because it's clear I have an anxious attachment style because I get stressed in close relationships. I find them scary and I get concerned about getting close to someone because I'm always scared they're going to

abandon me like everyone else in my life. Thankfully, this is something I'm actively working on and I recently learnt I have disorganised attachment as my main form of attachment too.

Thirdly, there is the "freeze" reaction where a client might passively detach themselves or zone out from a situation and find ways to avoid conflict. This leads the client to being impulsive, procrastinate and experience self-alienation.

Penultimately, a client might have an "attach" reaction where they are overwhelmed with a strong, painful need to be close to others but they're always stuck feeling lonely, sad and other people might call them emotionally needy and desperate.

This is something I can partly relate too as part of my attachment style because when I do find someone I want to be close to, and this is even more true when I'm struggling myself. Yet I used to get as close as possible to someone and I didn't want to be lonely and I did come across as emotionally needy.

Finally, a client might have a "feign or submit" reaction to other people where they only think about the other person's needs so they degrade or they become blind to their own needs. Or they feel guilty or criticise themselves for having needs of their own.

I won't say too much because as someone who regularly interacts with someone who fits this description. I understand that it's a trauma response and it is just something that they have learnt, but it is hurtful and almost "annoying" to see someone not recognise this when they're calling you out for your own attachment and boundary issues. Since when someone with a "feign or submit" reaction does recognise their own needs and they stop supporting the other person without warning because they didn't realise how much they were degrading their needs. It's hurtful and it really sucks.

How To Cope With Boundary Styles Using Positive Self-Talk?

As a result if we're ever working with a client who might fall into one of these five reactions, even though they are likely to have a single main or dominant reaction but still dip into the other types of boundary styles depending on the situation. It's important that we help clients to learn how best to cope with their boundary styles, in addition to any trauma work that needs to be done.

Therefore, there are three things that clients can do to help themselves with their boundary style. Firstly, they can use journaling with a sense of curiosity and control as a way to track their relationship patterns. I'll be the first to admit that you will be blind to your relationship patterns because they are so normal for you and you don't know anything else. As well as you often only realise that you have unhealthy relationship patterns because someone has pointed it out to you. Yet if a client doesn't have access to someone who will point it out to them, they can use journaling to identify their feelings around staying present with emotions in relationships. And clients could explore what not submitting or feigning would be like for them. Also, they could explore the thoughts and feelings that going against their boundary style brings up. So the client can ultimately find out what they are most afraid of when it comes to changing up their boundary style.

Secondly, it's critical that clients learn to trust their body. This was a major part of my sexual trauma counselling because your body, your senses and your nervous system are a brilliant tool to help you survive and it picks up on so much more information than you even realise. Yet your body is the first thing that will tell you when your boundary style is being triggered so you can trust your body and learn from it. For example, if you enter a certain situation and you start feeling dread, anxious and like you're going to get shouted at or punished. Then notice these signs and figure out where you learnt them based on your trauma. Then you can identify areas to work on.

For me, at times my boundary styles can be triggered when I get close to people because I'm scared they're going to hurt me, betray me and I'm going to lose everything again like I have in the past. I never want to go through all that pain, suffering and conflict ever again.

Finally, clients can use self-talk to cope with their boundary style because after a client has noticed and identified their triggers. They can start talking to themselves and instead of being your scared traumatised child self, they can show themselves compassion, love and attention as an adult that the client might never have received as a child.

Internal Family System Therapy is essentially built around this idea and I have some experience with a few techniques from this therapy because of my private counselling in 2023. I found it really helpful.

Conclusion

On the whole, when it comes to childhood trauma, or as I found out last night all forms of trauma, it will affect you in a million different ways. It will affect you from your relationships, your attachment styles, how you relate to others, your mental health, perhaps your ability to work and so many more areas.

However, just because childhood trauma causes you or your client to have a certain boundary style, doesn't mean you're messed up, you're doomed or you can't change. The traumatised part of yourself is still inside you, it will be scared of being close to others because you don't want to risk going through your childhood again. I understand that, and that's okay. It really is.

Nonetheless, you're an adult now. You don't need to depend on neglectful or abusive adults anymore, and what you really need, what that child part of you really needs, is for you to compassionately care for that child part. Provide it with the love, comfort and reassurance that you probably never received as a child.

Once you realise this you can and probably should work on it in therapy with a trained trauma informed mental health professional. They can help you work through your trauma and most importantly, how to safely manage your relationship boundaries so you can grow and thrive instead of just survive.

Here are some questions at the end of this psychology podcast episode:

- Have you ever experienced childhood trauma?
- Do you or anyone you know fit into one of these boundary styles?
- How could you identify any triggers or situations that activate your boundary styles?
- Could you find a mental health professional to help you work through this?

Child Psychology References and Further Reading

Erozkan, A. (2016). The Link between Types of Attachment and Childhood Trauma. *Universal journal of educational research*, *4*(5), 1071-1079.

Fisher, Janina (2017) Healing the Fragmented Selves of Trauma Survivors: Overcoming Internal Self-Alienation. Routledge.

Fuchshuber, J., Hiebler-Ragger, M., Kresse, A., Kapfhammer, H. P., & Unterrainer, H. F. (2019). The influence of attachment styles and personality organization on emotional functioning after childhood trauma. *Frontiers in psychiatry*, *10*, 643.

MacDonald, K., Sciolla, A. F., Folsom, D., Bazzo, D., Searles, C., Moutier, C., ... & Norcross, B. (2015). Individual risk factors for physician boundary violations: The role of attachment style, childhood trauma and maladaptive beliefs. *General Hospital Psychiatry*, *37*(5), 489-496.

Skinner-Osei, P., & Levenson, J. S. (2018). Trauma-informed services for children with incarcerated parents. *Journal of Family Social Work*, *21*(4-5), 421-437.

Valeras, A. B., Cobb, E., Prodger, M., Hochberg, E., Allosso, L., & VandenHazel, H. (2019). Addressing adults with adverse childhood experiences requires a team approach. *The International Journal of Psychiatry in Medicine*, *54*(4-5), 352-360.

Walker, Pete (2013) Complex PTSD: From Surviving to Thriving: A Guide and Map for Recovering from Childhood Trauma. CreateSpace Independent Publishing Platform.

Yilmaz, H., Arslan, C., & Arslan, E. (2022). The effect of traumatic experiences on attachment styles. *Anales de Psicología/Annals of Psychology*, *38*(3), 489-498.

BESTSELLING AUTHOR OF FORENSIC PSYCHOLOGY
CONNOR WHITELEY
SOCIAL MEDIA PSYCHOLOGY
A GUIDE TO CLINICAL PSYCHOLOGY, CYBERPSYCHOLOGY AND DEPRESSION

BESTSELLING AUTHOR OF FORENSIC PSYCHOLOGY
CONNOR WHITELEY
SUICIDE PSYCHOLOGY
A SOCIAL PSYCHOLOGY, COGNITIVE PSYCHOLOGY AND NEUROPSYCHOLOGY GUIDE TO SUICIDE

SUICIDE PSYCHOLOGY

A Social Psychology, Cognitive Psychology and Neuropsychology Guide To Suicide

INTRODUCTION

There is no easy way to talk about suicide and there are even fewer books on the topic.

In our society, it is almost a dirty word, a taboo topic and something that mustn't be addressed at all costs.

Not only are these societal and personal attitudes outrageous, wrong and disgusting, but they aren't helpful. As well as they create so many powerful myths and misconceptions that end up making suicide worse, and these myths kill people.

Whilst I fully admit this book tackles a difficult topic, it is actually written slightly differently to the rest of my psychology books. And this book is completely fact and evidence-based, but there are a lot of pieces of unofficially advice and tips in the book.

As well as in a way, this book is really written in a great, easy-to-understand way that's engaging and conversational (like all my books) for three different groups of people. But given how interconnected everyone actually is when it comes to suicide, everyone benefits from everything in this book.

Therefore, the vast majority of readers will undoubtedly be my normal audience of psychology students and professionals that want to deepen their knowledge of this topic.

As a result, this book covers so many amazing topics from myths about suicide to the risk factors and mental health to more nuanced topics like suicides amongst children, teenagers and young people.

In addition, maybe you suffered a recent loss to suicide and you're confused, worried and maybe feel a bit of guilt about it. This book helps you to understand that this is normal, it wasn't your fault and it helps to explain what actually could have happened to your loved one.

One of the entire points of this book is to help explain to everyone how suicide really works because most people just work off the awfully harming myths that are wrong. This book is designed and written to help people become more aware, learn what happened to their loved one and something else entirely.

In the case that someone is suicidal is reading this book, then of course get professional help **immediately**. But in case that seems too impossible right now, this helps to explain what's going on, how to talk to other people about what you're experiencing and why it is critical you get help immediately.

Personally, this entire book and every single word in it, is meant to help you as the reader. It is meant to help you learn more, become more aware and it might even save a life.

I don't know if this book will but I wrote it with the intention that I could save a life and help people.

Therefore, if you want a great, easy-to-understand book that has tons of references and research behind it (including the reference list at the end) that's written in a helpful, conversational and engaging tone then definitely buy this book.

And normally in these introductions, I introduce myself at a bit of length, but I don't want to keep you away from learning more about this critical and fascinating area.

Therefore, all I'll quickly say is I'm Connor Whiteley, an author of over 30 psychology books, a psychology student from the University of Kent, England and the host of The Psychology World Podcast available on all major podcast apps and YouTube with over 185 episodes looking at a wide range of psychology topics.

Now we know a bit more about each other, let's dive into this interesting, slightly tragic and fascinating area of psychology.

MALE SUICIDES: A SILENT CRISIS

For the first chapter of the book, I really wanted to start off with a sort of introductory chapter that looked at why suicide is such a critical topic to focus on. That's why this first chapter and some chapters after chapter three are drawn from podcast episodes of The Psychology World Podcast as this will help you to see my own journey of easing into this difficult topic before deciding to write this book.

Enjoy.

***

Male Suicides: A Silent Clinical Psychology Crisis

After wanting to do a psychology podcast episode for a while on suicide, I've finally felt like I'm ready to do one because this is a difficult topic for anyone, some more than others. Because no one wants to talk about suicide and I understand it because it is a "dark" topic. But that creates problems because people experiencing suicide ideation, don't feel like they can talk to anyone about it.

Therefore, the aim of this episode is to help shine some light on the psychology of suicide so we can all become more aware.

Male Suicides:

In the USA around 35,000 men commit suicide each year because of various factors and some of these we will look at today. In other words, in the USA that means 1 man kills themselves every 15 minutes.

In Canada, around 3,000 men die each year by suicide, over 50 men each week.

Also I know I'm only talking about men here and that's because in the USA 75% of suicides are done by men.

In addition the most concerning thing about this is that these rates are rising because the US Centers for Disease Control report found that suicide rates had increased by around 2% from 2006 to 2017. As well as this might not sound like a lot but it's actually a 26 percent increase from 1999.

Therefore, I just want to stop for a moment and… say how scary this is. Personally this scares me that so many men (and women) feel the need to commit suicide because their life has gotten so bad and they don't feel like they have any other option.

Additionally, I know a lot of people who have never experienced suicidal ideation can't fully understand it, and some even just call these people attention seekers. (That's outrageous) But as humans we are hard-wired to survive, live and pass on. What I'm trying to say here is no one *wants* to commit suicide for no reason.

These people feel like they *have* to commit suicide.

Inadequate Suicide Prevention Measures:

Before I talk about the next section, I want to mention that I am not discrediting, attacking or "slating" current suicide prevention services, what I am doing is commenting on them from a book called *Men's Issues and Men's Mental Health* by Springer that the book points out are core arguments about the existing approaches.

Also as I've mentioned on the podcast before, in psychology I love how we're always critically thinking so we can improve services so we can help people and make their lives better.

The first argument the book makes is about the narrow focus on the concept of masculinity and how it lacks any peripheral vision to look at the adverse social context experienced by many men.

Personally, I have always said this and this point extends into societal factors as a whole. Since traditionally men are meant to be strong, emotionless people who get on with male jobs, and they leave the women to be the emotional wrecks that society depicts them as.

This traditional view of men is useless,

extremely unhelpful and it is a major factor in male mental health, because of this societal view men don't want to come forward and get professional help. Due to getting professional help makes them look less manly, weak, pathetic and all that other rubbish that society thinks about men who want to better their lives.

Therefore, this traditional view of men does need to change.

Blaming, Shaming and Male Deficits:

This is another great point to make about suicides and this can be taken in two parts.

The first can be broadened to all suicides there is a blame and shame culture around suicide because I've heard of tons of comments from people from all walks of life blaming the person who committed suicide for their actions. But I want to come back to an earlier point because no one wants to kill themselves, there are factors in their life (both genetic and environmental) that make them feel like they have no other option.

So the fact that instead of looking at their life and blaming those factors, people feel the need to blame the person who killed themselves because they felt they had no other option.

This is just… sad, outrageous and awful that as a society we feel like it's okay to do that.

In addition, it is possible that this is one reason why people don't speak out that they're experiencing suicidal ideation because they don't want to be blamed for how they're feeling. As well as I mention this in different forms in various mental health episodes of the Podcast.

This is sadly nothing new.

However, on the flip side, there's blaming male mental health on alleged male deficits. For example, males are typically stubborn. I know some men are, but that is no excuse not to help people or not take their mental health seriously.

Male Friendly Services

Now this is an argument I've adopted from the references below because the friendliness of a mental health services towards a group of people is always a problem in clinical psychology, and this is where the problem with the lack of diversity within clinical psychology really shows itself.

Therefore, I want to hammer it home again because with the lack of male clinical psychologists from different backgrounds. It means that there aren't that many relatable people that men can have therapy with and build a therapeutic alliance.

Since men might not want to talk about their difficulties in front of a woman because they may believe they shouldn't look "weak" in front of the fairer sex. This is where a male therapist who they can relate with could be useful.

Conclusion:

Originally, I was going to go on to talk about more the nitty-gritty findings of suicides in men but I'll save that for another podcast episode.

Yet I do want to finish up by saying if you or someone you love is complementing suicide, please, please, please seek immediate help.

In the UK, you can contact *Samaritans* and *Mind.*

In the US, you can **use the 24/7 contact service at** the National Suicide Prevention Lifeline**, 1-800-273-TALK, or**

reach out to the Crisis Text Line by texting TALK to 741741.

If you're in a different country, please find your country's equivalent and get help.

MYTHS ABOUT SUICIDE

The reason why this is the second chapter in the book is simply because I want to tackle a lot of utterly stupid myths right now, just so we can get them out of the way and we can focus on facts.

Personally, I hate these myths with an utter passion because they are harmful, evil and just end up causing a lot more damage to people.

And the entire point of this book is to help raise awareness and maybe help people too.

To that end this chapter will look at 12 myths in varying amounts of detail just so moving forward we are all on the same page, and we can all interpret this information without seeing it through any myths.

As well as whilst I am extremely passionate about this area, I do completely understand if you believe any of these myths. They are so powerful in society and they could easily be considered cultural norms in their own right, they're that strong in people's minds. And I have believed some of these in the past but that's why I want, need to tackle these head on.

Suicide Myth 1

If you ask someone about suicidal thoughts, it may trigger them to act out.

I'll fully admit that a bunch of these myths we will focus on different sections of the book, and this one does pop up later.

However, for now just know that research shows that by asking someone about suicidal thoughts it will NOT put any ideas into their head that were not already in there. As well as suicidal people want to be asked about and they want to know they matter.

Asking out saves lives 99.9% of the time, so if you're concerned about someone, ask.

Suicide Myth 2

People who talk about suicide never do it.

Now this myth I do understand because in different areas of our social world, it is often the people that bang on about things are the ones that cannot do it. For example, the loudest people that praise how great they are, tend not to be as great as people who don't praise their own achievements.

Things like that.

However, when it's suicide, this is an extremely wrong myth and this easily causes deaths. Since when it comes to suicide, it is the people that do talk about it are the people most likely to do it. That's a major theme through this book.

Therefore, if someone does tell you they're going to self-harm or commit suicide, take it seriously and get them professional help.

Suicide Myth 3

Suicide is an impulsive act.

This is another myth that is completely wrong, and whilst there are sections of this book and research that sort of supports the idea of suicide is related to impulsivity. The vast, vast majority of suicides are planned down to the last detail and suicidal people think about committing suicide for days, weeks or even months before an attempt.

So no, suicide is flat out not an impulsive act and that thinking can harm people because it means others aren't looking out for the warning signs.

Suicide Myth 4

The elderly don't commit suicide.

I suppose in some weird way I can sort of see the twisted logic behind this myth because I think other people believe that because elderly people are, well, elderly they might just wait a few more years anyway to die of natural causes.

However, research shows that the elderly are most likely to complete suicide attempts successfully. And there are other factors that other groups don't always have.

Like losing friends and being alone because they've died, terminal illness, the pain and immobility associated with older age and more.

We all need to remember that suicide is not specific to one group. Suicide can happen to anyone, even if they're in a group with not a lot of extra risk factors.

Suicide Myth 5

Minorities are most likely to commit suicide.

Whilst this seems like a perfectly logical argument at first and it is true these minority groups have risk factors that make them more likely to commit suicide compared to others. It is actually white men that are the most likely to commit suicide due to a range of factors, most of which probably being down to men's inability to get professional help, because of personal and cultural factors as discussed in other chapters.

Suicide Myths 6

Young people aren't at risk of committing suicide. They only use it as a threat to get attention.

If there was one myth that was absolutely outrageous and made me bite my tongue because I wanted to swear so much, it would be this myth.

It is flat out outrageous, ridiculous and utterly pathetic that people dare to think suicide is an attention-seeking mechanism. It is these people that make talking about suicide and the stigma of suicide reinforced, stronger and make sure that people suffer in silence.

As you can tell I hate this myth because as future chapters will show you, it is young people that are *most* at risk of suicide. And by saying that young people are just being attention seekers is outrageous and I truly hope that these awful people realise the damage they are doing in the world by their ignorance.

If I have just insulted you, then I am sorry, and I actually do want to praise you because you are actively finding out more information and that's great. You want to learn and you are probably wanting to find out the truth, it is just a shame that more people aren't like you in this want.

Suicide Myth 7

There's nothing you can do if someone wants to commit suicide.

Personally I have absolutely no idea how this myth came about. I sort of think it may have come about as a way for loved ones, friends and others that learnt about someone's suicidal intent to wash their hands of them and simply not worry about them. And I suppose it could be a coping mechanism for dealing with this new revelation or loss of a loved one, but it is wrong.

Just because someone thinks they want to commit suicide does not mean they are a so-called *lost cause* (hate that idea). We'll talk about it later but there are tons of things you can do to help them, from telling them they are loved and supported, finding them professional help and telling them they are not worthless.

This is covered in a lot more depth in a future chapter, but I just needed to stress that things now.

Suicide Myth 8

Suicide victims always leave a note.

Maybe Hollywood, TV and books are to blame here for that myth but it is only roughly 25% of suicide victims that leave a note. And this unfortunately makes perfect sense because if you believe no one cares about you, you are isolated and lonely, then writing a note will seem truly pointless because you believe no one cares about you so why on earth would they care about reading some note.

Therefore, writing a note seems truly pointless when they already think no one cares about them and others would be better off with them dead.

So they don't do it.

I know it's "nice" to imagine they would leave a note to help give the family closure but that ideal just doesn't match up with the psychological state of suicidal people.

Suicide Myth 9

Anyone who attempts or commits suicide is depressed.

This is another myth I won't go into in too much depth because disproving this myth is basically a theme and one of the purposes of the book, so for now just know there is a wide range of factors that can increase a person's chance to commit suicide.

It is certainly not all down to depression.

Suicide Myth 10

If someone really wants to die we should let them.

I know the vast majority of people here would want to come at this myth from the viewpoint of *all lives are precious and must be saved,* and whilst that is one way to look at the myth.

Another way or reason why this is a myth is because a good amount of suicide survivors realise when they actually do the attempt that they have made a mistake. One great example of this is the author Kevin Hines who jumped off the Golden Gate Bridge, and realised he had made a mistake the second his feet left the concrete.

Final Suicide Myth

Suicide is selfish

I have definitely saved the best myth for last because I am fighting an extremely strong urge here to start swearing because I am so fed up with ignorant people daring to blame the suicide victims for their actions. I am fed up with the stupid beliefs of people who have never ever been suicidal thinking that their actions are rational and these suicide victims are being selfish.

For example, I know tons of people that I love and care about who believe suicidal people are selfish when they want to jump off bridges and the police close the roads.

But this is just outrageous and it shows such ignorance and uncaring towards people that are NOT thinking straight, rationally or see another way out.

No one wants to kill themselves for crying out loud, people only want to kill themselves when they see no other choice because of the wide range of factors.

If the suicidal person wanting to end their live disrupts your day then maybe that is a good thing, because it can only take one single person reaching out to possibly save a life, and not leave a family shattered.

Instead of people blaming the suicide victims for apparently being selfish (what utter rubbish), we need to address why are they feeling like they have no other choice. If it's a factor about society, like a LGBT person being scared about their future, then it is on all of us to take a hard look at ourselves, our neighbourhood and the world we live in to realise what can we do to make sure this doesn't happen again.

And if a person doesn't think suicides can happen again for the same reasons, then I'm sorry but that person needs this book desperately.

HOW SOCIAL FACTORS IMPACT MALE SUICIDE?

After looking at the extremely important topic of suicide myths which as you could tell from that chapter is a passionate area of mine, we need to return to talking about male suicide but in a slightly different way than before.

In this chapter, you'll start to get a sense of the wide range of causes of suicide and most importantly, how social factors impact suicide and what we can hopefully do to prevent it.

A chapter that is definitely worth a read.

***

How Social Factors Impact Male Suicide?

After looking at male suicide as a whole in episode 122, Where we learnt how suicide rates, the general psychology behind suicide and why it's increasing. We now need to investigate a new approach to treating and preventing male suicide. And this will be very eye-opening for all of us!

How Socials Factors Impact Male Suicide?

Like all mental health conditions, male suicide is caused by a number of different interacting factors, but social factors will be the focus of this episode. Simply because these are the factors that can be changed to create more user friendly services for men, building upon the last episode.

Furthermore, the following groups are most likely to be affected by male suicide:

- Unemployed Men
- Divorced Men
- Military Veterans
- Aboriginal Men
- Men with mental health conditions

In addition, the reason why we're looking at these groups of men is simple. For a lesser or greater extent, all these groups share the themes of social isolation, suspicion from wider society, financial strains amongst others. Not only does all this put an additional strain on their mental health, but all these factors can sadly result in wider society giving them a lack of empathy for one reason or another.

All meaning these groups of men are less likely to get the empathy and support they need.

Social Alienation:

This is a particularly awful social factor for everyone, but even more so for these groups of men. Due to when people experience a perceived or real rejection from society then this can lead to a strong sense of social alienation. Leading to the person feeling like they don't have a purpose or meaning in their life anymore.

Both of those are primary reasons for staying alive.

If we use a practical example, in most western countries (the US, UK, France, etc) men tend to get meaning from their lives from two sources. (And yes I know I'm being generic here but it shows the point perfectly)

They tend to get meaning and purpose from being in the workforce and being the centre (or head) of a family.

Therefore, when a man loses his family in a divorce or losses his job and becomes unemployed, this can put massive strains on their mental health. As the men could believe they don't have meaning or purpose in their life anymore.

Stereotypes and Male Suicide

Additionally, stereotypes that stigmatise individuals. Like aboriginal men, men with mental health conditions and veterans. These can have even more damaging consequences because these stereotypes lead to people not having as many opportunities for work or dating in the first place, so this leads them to not socially integrate and becoming marginalised.

Leading to social alienation again.

And this is why I hate with a passion stereotypes because most of them are so completely wrong, so they only do more damage for no flaunt of the sufferer. For example, the stupid myth about everyone with a mental health condition is dangerous or depressed people are just lazy.

No!

But hopefully over time these myths, lies and stereotypes will get less and less powerful.

What Does This Mean For Prevention Programmes?

Now we know the information, how do we apply it to the real world and hopefully try to save lives?

If we're going to talk about a new or renewed approach to help prevent male suicide. Then the programme would have to do at least three things.

Firstly, just like the principles of Formulation, we would have to tailor-make the therapy or support to the male in particular. Therefore, the man would get tailored support to their needs to make sure the transition they're undergoing is as easy as possible. Like in a divorce or them becoming unemployed.

Secondly, like I talk about in Abnormal Psychology Third Edition, the psychotherapy or support would have to be adapted to become cultural appropriate since that works best (check out the book for studies). For example, you would have to adapt the therapy given to Aboriginal men in a different way to military veterans to make sure the therapy is as effective as possible.

Finally, the overall mental health service (which is somewhat broken as it due to budget cuts, the focus on the biomedical model and other factors) definitely has a role to play. Since research shows that men prefer grassroots services and local programmes for their mental health, so support through be developed through local services.

Some of these grassroots places include spiritual or religious organisations, local peer-to-peer support groups and other non-profits. As well as these organisations are actually well placed to help with mental health, the feelings of social alienation and loss of meaning and purpose in life.

Wrap Up

After covering the basics of male suicide, I know that there is a lot that needs to change in the world before the silent crisis of male suicide can start to slow down, and hopefully stop one day. But I really hope by talking about the psychology of suicide on the podcast, I can start to educate people about it. (And educate myself too)

In the following suicide-based podcast episodes, we'll start to look at the really interesting aspects of suicide and cover aspects I had no idea were related to suicide. So fascinating episodes ahead!

But please, if you, your friends or anyone you know ever thinks about suicide, please seek professional help.

HOW DOES DEPRESSION IMPACT SUICIDE?

Whilst a lot of this book will focus on mental health and other wide ranging factors that can increase the chance of people committing suicide, before we go any further we need to at least be introduced to the topic of mental health.

Therefore, this is another podcast episode from early in 2022 that focuses on depression and how that impacts suicide by focusing on 3 questions surrounding the topic.

How Does Depression Impact Suicide? 3 Questions Answered

After looking at suicide already in a lot of depth, we need to consider how depression affects suicide. Since as always there are a lot of myths and misconceptions about how depression impacts suicide, so in this psychology podcast episode, that is exactly what we seek to look at. How does Depression impact suicide?

How Does Depression Impact Suicide?

How Does Depression Lead To Suicidal Thinking?

Lots of different people experience suicidal thinking in their life and this usually happens after a difficult life event. Like the loss of a loved one, job or something else that is important to them, as we've spoken about on previous episodes.

In addition, depression links to this type of thinking because it impairs our cognitive flexibility as it changes our patterns of feeling and thinking so we cannot see a way out of our current situation. As well as we cannot imagine or even entertain the idea of a better future.

Also the Cognitive Triad in depression leads a person to focus on all their setbacks, all their so-called mistakes and what makes them a failure. Including relationship failures and adverse childhood experiences. Therefore, this only adds to their feelings of worthlessness and depression that only magnifies the pain they're suffering.

All leading to a depressed person being more likely to seek out suicide as the only viable escape route from all this suffering and psychological pain.

Personally, this is rather tragic to write about but it is important. It is important for all of us to understand the importance of treatment and the work we do as psychology professionals and in the future psychology students. It is the work we do that can save lives, or at the very least help people decrease and cope with their psychological distress.

This is why psychology is critical.

How Common Is Suicide In Depression?

According to the U.S Department of Health and Human Services, it turns out 2% of people who are treated for depression in an outpatient service take their own life. As well as out of all those people who were ever hospitalised for depression, the death rate by suicide is 4%.

Before I go on to dive into the numbers a

bit more, I just wanted to mention that this does sort of fly in the face of a massive misconception about suicide. Since I have heard plenty of times through the grapevine so to speak that people believe that all depressed people commit suicide.

Thankfully that is far, far, far from the case. But still 4% is too high for my liking. It should be 0% in an ideal world and thankfully that is where psychologists come in.

Additionally, around 60% of suicide victims have a mood condition that is potentially treatable and younger people who kill themselves often have a substance abuse difficulty as well. Of course, in addition, to the other life factors that can impact suicide.

And this is the main reason why I talk about all these things in my books, in-person and on the podcast. Because even if I can educate or prompt one person to convince others to get professional help if they have a mental health condition, then that means I could have potentially saved a life.

This is why psychologists and therapists are critical because without us so many people would still be suffering.

As well as this is why I hate with a passion all the rubbish that psychology gets. With people thinking we know nothing, psychology is profiling and therapists are dangerous (as in villains in TV and books). Because this bad representation isn't helpful to us, our clients and the people who need professional aid but don't trust us.

Anyway jumping off my soapbox now!

Do Anti-Suicide Pacts Work?

Wow!

This is actually rather cool and rather clever.

So these pacts have been around for ages between at-risk patients and therapists as a way to stop the patient from committing suicide. These pacts or contracts can be written or verbal but that isn't important. What is important is that it gets the at-risk patient to not self-harm or commit suicide.

As well as the pacts make the patient call the therapist, an emergency number or 999 if they even think about suicide for a moment.

Furthermore, effective suicide contracts which are written, dated and signed with a copy given to each person and kept in an accessible location. Not only ensure the patient doesn't kill themselves but it ensures they call emergency numbers when they're in danger.

Again what is so brilliant about these pacts is they are not legally binding so that increases comfort for the patient. As the therapist cannot and does not need to file it in court and get the patient arrested. Because of course, suicide is a crime.

Also this is already very commonplace in certain industries where the suicidal rates are extremely high. Like in paramedics and other first responders, with them becoming more and more common amongst friends and family members of anyone who has been suicidal.

And this is what I love about this podcast, because I think this pact is utterly amazing. It is such an effective and easy to do method that I'm extremely pleased that people have this option.

Conclusion:

After today's episode, I'm actually… rather hopeful about the future because if this episode has taught me anything. It is how important psychology students (for the future) and psychology professionals are, because we are a massive line of defence for depressed people.

Also I guess that was the real point for today's episode, it was to teach all of us how valuable we are for depressed people, and why our work matters so much to so many.

And I have to admit I love those anti-suicide pacts. I think they're a great idea. Of course, nothing on the podcast is ever official advice, but they're still pretty great.

SUICIDE AND PRISONS

If you've ever listened to my podcast or any other of my books then you know that I love forensic psychology in its own right and as a subfield of clinical psychology, so I suppose that it would be impossible for me not to look into how forensic psychology and suicide overlapped.

And in terms of this book, I wanted to change our perspective a little, just so we're looking at something completely different before we dive into other topics.

You seriously cannot get further away from the things we have previously looked at (to some extent) than looking at suicidality in criminals.

Enjoy.

***

Stepping away from clinical psychology and looking at suicide through that lens, we now need to look at how the forensic psychology of suicide by looking at criminals and suicide. I have spoken about this in my Forensic Psychology book, but in today's podcast episode we're going to look at it from another angle. This is going to be really, really interesting!

Suicide and Prisons

There are two "danger zones" for suicide when it comes to criminals. The first is when they are arrested and taken to jail at the police station or something like this before they go to prison. As well as the second danger zone is when they go to prison itself.

Both of these situations and places are suicidal danger zones (especially in the first 24 hours) because the criminal's future looks so uncertain to them. And as we spoke about in the last podcast episode on suicide, is that uncertainty about the future and inability to see a better one, that leads to suicidal ideation. Then the attempt itself.

As a result, this is why suicide rates in prisons are extremely high compared to the outside world.

But besides from the lack of a certain future, what other factors increase the risk of suicide in prisons?

Crying Wolf:

Now of course the crying wolf title isn't anything official but it is an easy way to imagine what the research shows. For example, we have all seen at least once or twice a TV programme or film where the prisoner screams about their in pain, they need to see a doctor or they're going to kill themselves if something doesn't happen. Then if someone does help them then they are attacked and the prisoners escape.

In reality, this rarely happens but because it is overly used in Television. It sort of becomes part of our collective knowledge so we expect it to happen. This doesn't help the situation, especially considering what I say below.

This does happen in the real world and

sadly there are inmates that fake real suicide ideation. Leading to the prison officers to conclude that all prisoners are simply crying wolf and are lying. Meaning no prison officers are going to help them.

Personally I can understand this because even the most compassionate prison officers can become immune to these cries for help. And then if you read into forensic psychology and the workplace culture of prisons, then you learn that it is understandable for the officers not to be too helpful towards the inmates. Unfortunately.

Hardening Officers:

As I mentioned in the above section, over time as a compassionate and hopeful new prison officer gets to experience prisoners and what work is actually like inside a prison. This can lead to them hardening their attitudes towards the inmates making them harsher, stricter and generally less likely to believe them and this affects their judgements too.

Again I do understand this because it isn't easy working in a prison. And you must have to deal with some truly horrible people on the more extreme end of the scale. Then again, you get to work with some good people too that have simply made a bad choice.

But as we know from Cognitive and Social Psychology, we always tend to remember the bad more than the good.

In addition, it is terrible that "just dessert" sentiments flow free in our society. Meaning even if a prison officer believes the criminal will commit suicide they may not bother trying to prevent it, because it is what they deserve.

Prolonged Sentences:

A final reason for suicide in prisons can be linked to inmates who are serving a prolonged prison sentence. For example, a life sentence or a whole life sentence. As this prolonged length of prison time can make inmates think that suicide is a reasonable reaction to such a sentence. And interestingly people on the outside believe it too.

Of course there are more people that serve long prison sentences and do not commit suicide, but depression and suicidality are common like we spoke about before.

What Is Done?

All prisons have different processes in place for suicidal inmates but there are problems with everything. For example, in one place if an inmate was seen to be suicidal, they would have their cell stripped of every single thing that could be used to end themselves with. Even their sheets and mattress, so the inmate was given a strange foam thing to cover themselves with at night.

But inmates can still climb up on their sink and jump. That's all I'm going to say about that.

In addition, if suicidal inmates don't stop in their ideation then they can be moved to hospitals for treatment. And lots of other complicated and unfortunately bureaucratic processes can happen too.

However, what is interesting is Joseph H. Baskin, M.D says that impulsivity suicidal inmates are actually easier to work with because they want to be helped and regarded. So it might be easier to reach out, form a therapeutic relationship and help them.

But still, the combination of hopelessness and impulsivity is deadly.

Conclusion:

Forensic psychology will always be one of my favourite areas of psychology. But this is both a fascinating and tragic topic to look at, because retribution doesn't get us anywhere so these "just dessert" sentiments are deadly. And even though these people have made bad choices, it doesn't mean they need to commit suicide.

So hopefully in the future more can be done to help prevent this, and decrease the alarmingly high suicide rate amongst prisoners.

STIGMA AND SUICIDE

To finish up the introductory content and before we move onto completely new content, I really wanted to share with you a reflection from my Clinical Psychology Reflections Volume 3 book because in that book I reflect a little on suicide, stigma and clinical psychology.

At best, I really hope this gives the book a bit more depth and it helps give you a new perspective.

At worse, I hope you enjoy this reflection.

***

Stigma and Suicide

I've been wanting to do this reflection for a rather long time now but I have just never felt ready to reflect on such a topic, but given how I'll be writing a psychology of suicide book at some point this year, I thought this would be a good way to dive into the topic.

And sometimes you just need to get on and actually do something, like this reflection.

Of course, there are a lot of different angles to look at when it comes to suicide but I really want to focus on the stigma angle.

In addition, I want to mention first of all that when a person decides to try and commit suicide. They don't want to do it, but they feel like they have absolutely no other choice, they've been abandoned by everything they love and they feel like a burden to their loved ones and friends.

And this is actually something that really, really annoys me about people when it comes to talking about suicide. Since if there is a jumper or someone learns about a person who has committed suicide, they tend to be indifferent or blaming the victim.

To some extremely limited extent, I can sort of "understand" where they are coming from. Since if you're driving to work or coming back from work and the authorities close the motorway (or highway for our international audience) because someone is going to jump off the bridge.

Then I can sort of see how that would be annoying and make the drivers angry because apparently the jumper is being selfish about their choice to kill themselves.

Thus, blaming the suicide victim for their behaviour.

Furthermore, the whole conversation in society about how selfish suicide is as a way to die is rather… no, extremely unhelpful because again it is blaming the victim. It is blaming the victim for not doing certain things, not being strong enough and all that other societal rubbish that makes mental health sufferers feel like they cannot reach out or get help.

However, the biggest problem with all of these victim blaming arguments is that they assume that a suicidal person is just as rational, logical and psychologically stable as the non-suicidal people that are blaming them.

But they aren't.

Due to if evolution and our biology has taught us anything, it is how badly humans are wired to survive. Humans are an innate drive to live and survive no matter what, so for a person to overcome our most primal instinct, it's bad.

No one wants to commit suicide, no one wants to end their life but suicidal people feel like they have absolutely no choice that the world is better off without them.

I have no idea how non-suicidal people think that screams logical, rational or psychologically stable. Because it flat out doesn't.

And this just goes to show how little people care or want to help suicidal people because if they did then they would at least have the common sense to realise that they do need psychological help. And they shouldn't be blamed.

You only need to research into the reasons why people want to kill themselves to know how wide ranging it is. From mental health to financial reasons to relationship problems and more. There is no such thing as a typical suicidal person, but they all need psychological help and people to support them.

Additionally, in the UK, because our governments are kept cutting back on mental health services for services and they are failing to get our services back in working order. Our mental health services do not have the time, money or resources to help people until they are suicidal.

Meaning if someone is depressed or suffers from another mental health condition and they come into a mental health service wanting help. Most of the time the NHS has to turn them away until it is a lot worse.

So when that same person tries to commit suicide a few months later, everyone in clinical psychology knows we should have seen that person months ago, but because of the state of the NHS and the lack of political will to do anything about it. This cycle of turning away people and leaving them to get worse will only continue.

Of course, none of these reflections are ever meant to be negative or I always like to put a positive spin on them towards the end. But I'm afraid even I can't be positive on a topic like this, because it is simply ridiculous that us as a society we are blaming people who are suicidal. When in actual fact we should be blaming the system that is failing us as future or current psychologists, and failing them.

And to make matters worse, this mental health crisis will only get worse and worse as time goes on. The mental health crisis was really bad before the pandemic, but the backlog of referrals only spiralled out of control during the COVID-19 pandemic.

Therefore, whilst it is flat out not our fault or the fault of our clients, something needs to be done.

Personally, this is why I'm looking forward to writing my book on the psychology of suicide just so I can see possible routes for the future, and how to prevent suicide. As well as I also hope that there will be structural changes within the NHS to help these problems and there will be a political change just so our politicians do start investing and caring about mental health and suicide more.

There is a lot to do, and I really hope something changes soon.

HOW TO TALK ABOUT SUICIDAL THOUGHTS?

Now that we have the basic information done, I just really, really want to put this chapter next because it is so critical. This is very much one of the most important chapters in this entire book, because before now and later in the book, I will mention how important it is for reaching out to loved ones and suicidal people.

But how on earth do you do that?

And I need to stress upfront that this chapter is for BOTH people considering suicide and for people who are concerned about a loved one. It is written with both groups of people in mind, and of course nothing in this book is never any sort of official advice.

I'm writing it that way because I don't want anyone to perceive me as making it sound easier than it is, because it really isn't. And I don't want people without suicidal experience to underestimate how difficult these conversations are.

Therefore, let me be very extremely clear here, talking about suicidal thoughts is extremely difficult for everyone involved and this widespread discomfort stems from our cultural norms. Since we still sadly live in a society where you simply do not talk about suicide because it is a taboo subject.

A subject that because it is taboo costs lives. Hence why I'm writing this book in the first place.

In addition, talking about suicidal thoughts as the person who has them or is concerned about a loved one, is a deeply emotionally painful experience to consider suicide.

It's painful for the person to suicide committing suicide because they feel that hopeless.

It's painful for the person concerned about a loved one, because no one likes to imagine their loved one feeling like this.

As a result, you might not know how to bridge the conversation and make these feelings come to light. This is a perfectly normal reaction and it really does not make you a bad person for feeling like this.

In fact, it's natural as the vast majority of people are hesitant to talk about this topic as well as people with suicidal thoughts may quit the idea of having this conversation out of fear of burdening loved ones.

Which is not correct, you are not a burden as you'll see later on in the chapter.

Additionally, the silence in our society only maintains the stigma and pushes those people with these suicidal thoughts into further isolation.

However, being willing to bridge the subject could help someone at risk towards very much needed help and start their journey towards emotional recovery. That's why this chapter is so important because it is so powerful.

And as always and as we're focusing on the powerful conversations, it is always better to reach out and maybe save a life than stay silent and risk a death.

Furthermore, anyone who is suspecting that a close other is thinking about suicide should talk to them but this is of course easier said than done. This is what we need to focus on now.

Since starting off this conversation can definitely seem impossible, because you will feel anxious and apprehensive at the idea. Suicidal people will feel like this because they're seeing the situation through their feelings of sadness, feeling worthless and being a burden with their loved ones being better off without them.

Concerned people will feel like this because they're scared of finding their fears are true, but they love the suicidal person and want to help them.

How To Talk About Suicidal Thoughts For People Concerned About A Loved One?

As well as it's important to note that actually talking about it in an open way and honest way is one of most powerful weapons to fight against it, and it's key to understanding that someone is struggling more than loved one can ever imagine.

Also there's decades of research that shows social support and suicide makes one thing clear, when in doubt, reach out.

Another helpful tip about approaching this topic could be to write some conversation tips down beforehand and this is a way to help manage anxiety and make you feel more in control. The exact same goes for formulating a plan and feeling empowered to start the conversation.

Moreover, it has to be mentioned that you certainly don't need to be a trained psychologist or mental health professional to start the conversation, just make sure after the conversation you help them connect with mental health services. But it might be a great idea to learn about risk factors and more about suicide, and as you're reading this book I hope you're okay on that front.

At the end of the day, you do not need to say the perfect thing and you won't be able to solve everything in one conversation, yet reaching out will help your loved one feel understood and it's likely the first step to recovery. And it could save their life further down the road.

Additionally, as we know from the second chapter, asking about suicide doesn't put the idea in their head, it's a myth, and a vast body of literature shows open conversations are unlikely to increase suicidal ideation.

It actually has the immense power to decrease it, especially when done with empathy and coupled with additional mental health support.

If after starting the conversation and if the loved one admits thoughts of hurting themselves, experts stress don't act shocked or horrified as this only creates distance and could make the loved one feel judged.

That isn't what you want.

Also it might be tempting to jump straight to problem-solving, but at this point it's important to see and listen without judgement and be empathic. As well as make an effort to validate their feelings. For example, by even saying something like, "I'm so sorry you're feeling so hopeless—it must be horrible" can be very powerful.

What you absolutely mustn't do is say they have no reason for feeling this way. That is flat out stupid, it will only reinforce the idea that no one cares about them, they're worthless and the world is better off without them.

Do not do that.

Afterwards this, it is absolutely critical to connect them with mental health support services.

Sharing Suicidal Thoughts With Others

This is extremely hard, I know, and it takes such immense amounts of courage to do this but it is critical, and in many cases such worries that the suicidal person has are far from true with many people they're close with are willing and able to help if only given the chance.

It is hard to reach out that is absolutely no denying that and if anyone says it is easy, then they are lying. Plain and simple. But no one is alone in this world and it is does not matter how dark the world seems with horrible people, wars and situations that seem impossible to escape from. There will always be people who are looking to help, support and care about you.

You are never alone.

This sharing does require a massive act of courage, and it is a valuable, if not critical, first step towards getting help and restoring your well-being. It is helpful to try to be as direct as possible, tell them how you're struggling with feelings of hopelessness, depression, worthlessness and any other things you're feeling.

The person you're telling might become emotional or respond with shock, and this will be a shock to you too because this might not be the reaction you wanted. This is why preparing ahead of time for any possible reaction can help you maintain composure and continue this conversation.

Continuing is just critical.

Then tell them what you need. Like help finding a therapist? Wanting them to be there for you? Listening to your challenges and offer emotional support.

At the end of the day, your loved ones care about you, and they may need to let others know about this, but please don't be frustrated with them because they are only doing what they believe is best for you.

It's valuable to take some time to prepare for this sort of conversation because this will help you to soothe your anxiety or any guilt in you, and this could allow you to become more proactive.

Yet if it is easy for you to get lethal means or the suicidal thoughts become persistent, do not prepare, just get help. Have the conversation.

However, sometimes it is too uncomfortable or you're unable to talk to loved ones because you actually know they won't respond well, or they believe you have no reason to feel like this.

Then DO NOT lose hope either.

Instead there are a lot of great suicide prevention hotlines that you can call for free, confidential help and they can provide emotional support and concrete assistance in getting more help for you.

Of course, no one can ever force anyone to share their thoughts with others, but many people who reach out to loved ones end up having a very worthwhile experience. Since struggling with suicidal thoughts is extremely isolating, and social connection can be a powerful source of comfort and relief.

And while it is true that sharing thoughts will lead others to worry, just like how you would be worried if they said the same to you. But we all forget sometimes that worry isn't about being a burden, it is a sign of love and that they care about you and want you to do well.

None of us worry about things we don't care about, so if your loved ones worry about you then that's a good sign. Because they love you and you aren't a burden.

It is best to share your thoughts, struggles and feelings regardless of your loved one's penchant for worry, and remember you're in control of what you share and how you share it.

Interestingly, if you're worried about how they'll respond, it can be helpful to have the conversation over phone or email, rather than face to face.

Do whatever allows you to share your thoughts and get what you need without focusing excessively on how others are responding emotionally.

And if you don't feel safe about sharing and reaching out, it is a great shame that some people don't respond well, so please reach out to a friend instead and if that's not possible, then reach out to a trusted community member. They may be able to provide emotional support and connect you with resources.

And remember sharing is critical in the journey to recovery and suicide hotlines are critical.

I'll repeat it. Suicide hotlines are critical.

WHAT ARE THE SIGNS SOMEONE IS THINKING ABOUT SUICIDE?

In a way I fully admit it might have made more sense to put this chapter before the last one, but personally I just really, really wanted to put the talking about suicide chapter as soon into the book as possible. And in a way, now that we know how to talk and the importance of the signs, this chapter seems a bit more relevant now.

Especially as the last chapter basically proved that it is possible to talk to suicidal people.

Therefore, spotting the signs that someone is thinking about committing suicide is uniquely challenging, and this only highlights the fact that when someone does lose a loved one to suicide, it doesn't mean they were bad parents, family members or they or the therapist was derelict in their duty.

It's hard to spot or recognise the signs.

It is also slightly helpful in this case that some people thankfully vocalise their intentions and externally show what they intend to do before they actually do it. Other people sadly conceal and hide their intentions, so it is a lot harder to recognise the signs.

In addition, it is flat out impossible to know what's going on in a person's head, none of us are mind readers. Yet it is always a good idea to ask if you see any warning signs or you suspect that the loved one might be thinking about suicide. Better safe than sorry.

And it is always better safe than sorry. Better to ask and get them to look at you funny and confused about why you would ask them. Then ask not, and lose them forever.

In terms of warning signs, there are a lot of common ones that you can watch out for. Of course, this will never be a complete list but some of these might be very useful to you in the future or right now.

If a person makes a will, tries to get "their affairs in order" and gives away personal possessions then this on its own might not be a warning sign, but when coupled with other signs, it is.

Secondly, if your loved one talks about feeling worthless, trapped, hopeless and like they have no reasons to keep living. And this is why it was important to have the last chapter first, because if you come across this particular warning sign then you know how to breach the topic.

Thirdly, if the loved one sleeps too little or too much that could be a sign of depression and other mental health conditions, and if they eat too much or too little. As well as if they have attempted suicide or shown suicidal behaviour in the past, then that is a clear warning sign they could do it in the future.

In addition, if they search for ways to harm themselves, then that is cause for concern. For example, if they search how to buy a gun or access dangerous medication, as well as if the loved one shows signs of despair or they have significant mood swings.

Here are some other warning signs:

- Have experienced a severe life stressor recently. For example, the death of a spouse or other loved one, the loss of a job or a traumatic event.
- Drinks alcohol or uses drugs excessively.
- Avoids other people, including loved ones; spends more time than usual alone.
- Acts agitated, anxious, or aggressive.
- They behave recklessly.

Of course, it needs to be mentioned that absolutely none of these are perfect indicators, but these are common signs within suicidal people, and they are critical to watch out for.

Are You At Risk Of Suicide?

One of the points of the book is try and be as honest with everyone as possible, and cater for different groups of people. And this is where the honesty comes in, because it turns out that most people at some point in their life will experience passing suicidal thoughts. Even if it is as simple as you being really furious with someone and you thinking *I wish I had never been born.*

If this thought happens then just bear in mind the predictors and try to manage your thoughts, like always focus on the positive.

However, if these suicidal thoughts stop becoming so passing and they become persistent. Then definitely take them seriously, as well as anytime they become noticeable or concerning, definitely seek help.

As a result of even if the person doesn't have a plan for suicide when these thoughts occur, a sudden spike in suicidal thinking likely suggests a larger mental health difficulty or a life challenge that can be productively addressed if you seek help.

And as always there is absolutely no shame in seeking help. It doesn't make you weak, silly or anything else that societal rubbish teaches us about mental health not being real health. I hate it when people preach those lies.

Additionally, even if the person's suicidal ideation hasn't shifted or moved from passive (thinking about committing suicide) to active (planning and making preparations for it), it's still a good idea to talk to a loved one or a therapist about these thoughts. Due to this is the first step to overcoming them, strengthening your mental well-being and starting a journey of recovery.

Also, it's worth noting that many people in psychotherapy with different mental health conditions are scared about telling their therapists that they have these suicidal thoughts.

Some of these fears are rather logical in a way because they are scared about their friends and family being told, and they're concerned about immediately being committed to an in-patient programme and they won't be able to go home that day.

However, please rest assured that mental health professionals are trained to handle these discussions without judgement or rash action. Meaning the fears are unfounded and this is a good thing that the client wants to tell the therapists.

Also a good therapist responds to this conversation with compassion and calm to make the whole experience better for the client. And as I always say, in clinical psychology, our job is to work with our clients to decrease their psychological distress and improve their lives.

Acting with compassion and calm is one of the ways we can do that.

Finally, in reality, in most cases the client is asked a few follow-up questions to help the therapist understand what's going on. For example, they probably be asked whether their suicide is in the passive or active stage, do they have a specific plan and do they have a readily accessible means of suicide.

After if the therapist concludes that the client isn't at an immediate risk, then they will likely work with them to develop a safety plan in case the thoughts escalate to an attempt. Meantime, in the therapy sessions the psychotherapist and client will explore the source of the suicidal thoughts and help to develop alternative coping mechanisms for the feelings of despair as well as hopelessness.

But the entire point of the chapter is two-fold. Firstly, even though there are not perfect indicators of suicidal intent, there are plenty to be aware of just in case.

And secondly, if you ever feel like you have passing thoughts of suicide, monitor them and make sure you get help if they become persistent.

HOW LGBT HATE CRIMES LINK WITH SUICIDE?

After the past few rather heavy chapters, I wanted to do a sort of lighter chapter in a way. Because whilst all suicide chapters are not positive in the slightest, this chapter has a more hopeful tone that definitely helped me to feel better after the past few chapters.

Personally I strongly believe this would be an absolutely awful book on suicide if we covered a lot of other things and not the high rate of LGBT deaths. This is something that scares me, I hate that people do not accept people from the LGBT community and there are places in the world were LGBT people feel so scared that they see suicide as their only option.

This is common and just flat out outrageous and I hate the findings of this chapter more than I could ever put into words.

On the off chance that an LGBT person is reading this chapter, all I can say is I know how scary the world seems at times and how much hate we can get, but you are loved and you are never alone.

How Hate Crimes Link With Suicide?

Moving onto the very important content, hate crimes, to oversimplify, are crimes done against a particular community or group of people and are designed to terrorise them, and are motivated by the offender's hate for that group.

In addition, the reasoning behind hate crime laws is twofold. Since the first reason for these laws is because the crimes are motivated by prejudice and hate, as well as they are especially harmful because they are designed to terrorise an entire community, not just direct victims.

Which is definitely a major way in how they differ from "normal" crimes. Typically crimes are designed to harm direct victims. Like the shoplifting only really hurts the shop owners, not the entire community of shop owners. But hate crimes don't work like that.

Secondly, the victims of these hate crimes are typically people from protected classes, with these being populations that have suffered and continue to suffer victimisation and discrimination.

Therefore, these crimes are committed against specific groups of people because of their minority status. Resulting in additional psychological harm to them, and this is both above and beyond the criminal harm per se.

Furthermore, whilst the political issue hate legislation is a question of public values and policy, and a whole bunch of other utterly ridiculous things that can stop these protective laws from coming into force.

What we're interested in is the scientific question about work of connecting hate crimes to harm and this can be pursued in a variety of innovative research methods. Since it's all well and good wanting to bring in hate crime laws, but what's the point if hate crime doesn't harm people?

Hence the need to research them and find out if hate crimes does actually harm people from minority groups.

As a result, this work brings together scientists from a wide range of areas. Such as teams from public health, sociology, criminology, psychology and others.

Just like professor Dustin Duncan at Harvard and now New York University, who lead a team of researchers interrogating the question of whether anti-LGBT hate crimes does harm the mental health of LGBT community. With their particular focus being on adolescents because this is the group with the highest suicide rate. Especially with the acceptance of being LGBT is a difficult time.

To do this the researchers examined at a number of levels, but Dr Ducan looked at the community-level data. More specifically the researchers mapped the reports of anti-LGBT hate crimes through the Boston area, and looked at the correlation between those hate crimes and suicide attempts by adolescents in the Boston area.

The results found that in "hot spot" areas of anti-LGBT bias and hate, there was an increased level of suicidality among LGBT youth.

This was confirmed by the analysis showing that poor mental health outcomes were specific to LGBT adolescents in these areas, not just young people overall. Due to that's a very important finding, because with research we can say that hate crime does increase suicide levels within the targeted community, and not the general population. Hence the need for hate crime laws.

As well as if we want to get very technical about these results, the public health terms for this is we would say the correlation is specific, not spurious.

Finally, because I promised a slightly more positive chapter at the start, I want to stress here to both LGBT people and non-LGBT people some things.

If you're not LGBT and these results don't affect you then I'm really pleased, and I would definitely encourage you to always be aware of this issue, challenge hate crimes and support minority groups. Because as we know from other chapters, the lack of support and hopelessness leads to suicide, and everyone can help prevent that if we confront it head on.

If you are LGBT then please know that things can get better. You can have an amazing life filled with love, respect and whatever you want. You are not deranged, possessed or whatever else the bible-bashers want to call you. You are an amazing person that is capable of so much and you are never ever alone.

There's a reason why LGBT is called a community. Sure it is hard to find sometimes, but there is a community that will love, support and respect you for sure.

There is always another way.

WHAT IS THE SUICIDE RISK OF CHILDREN, TEENAGERS AND YOUNG PEOPLE?

Whilst this might be the tenth chapter for you to enjoy, this is actually the last chapter for me because I felt the massive need to write this last. Personally I don't know why but after writing the rest of the book, I now know how critical this chapter is to the rest of the book.

Therefore, whilst I fully agree with you that this is a heart-wrecking topic. It is just so critical to fully understanding suicide, why people do it and helping to fight some of the absolutely outrageous myths that suicide makes up.

Let's begin.

As you can imagine the very idea of a child dying by suicide is simply unimaginable to many parents. It stirs up such a range of emotions and it can still people with such crippling grief.

However, a significant number of children do seriously think or attempt suicide, and this is one of the leading causes of death in children and teenagers. As well as whilst the evidence thankfully suggests that suicide is rare, it is becoming more common place.

As a result of this evidence, parents need to be aware of the key warning signs (there is a section dedicated to this later in the book), knowing what behavioural changes to look for, how to ask and how to find support for these children and teenagers. Which is something we have all looked at in this book together.

And it's important to know that this knowledge isn't meant to be scary, it's meant to be empowering for families, because with this knowledge families can provide emotional support to their child, know how to respond to their needs and put them on the road to recovery.

But I know I have mentioned throughout the book, and I will keep saying this, but if a child does commit suicide, it flat out doesn't mean the parents were bad.

There are a lot of non-parental risk factors.

<u>More Introduction:</u>

In my research this section was a little further down but I needed to bring it up here to give it the most impact.

Therefore, Janiri et al. (2020) found that 8% 9-to-10 year olds reported experiencing past or current suicidal thoughts with slightly more than 1% of this age group attempting suicide. As well as other research suggests that roughly 1 in 8 children between 6 and 12 experience suicidal thoughts.

And whilst it is completely impossible for us to think about this, children as young as five have been known to experience suicidal thoughts and small number of these young children die each year by suicide.

Furthermore, another study Bridge et al. (2015) found that less than 2 in every million children between 5 and 11 die by suicide. Yet Adolescents older than 12 die by suicide a rate of approximately 52 per million.

Overall, whilst this is extremely distressing to think about, it is just critical to remember that the risk is real, and very small. And none of this chapter is meant to scare parents or people who want to become parents in the future.

Parents can mitigate any potential danger by taking seriously any talk from their child about death, feeling like a burden, self-harm or feeling hopeless. Also it's important to talk to children about their feelings and fears, as well as making it clear that the parents are available whenever the child needs help, and if necessary, the parents are proactively seeking mental health care if their child needs it.

What Children Are At Risk?

Of course it is worth reminding ourselves that despite the evidence that child suicide is coming more common, in the grand scheme of things most children don't commit suicide, so the overall risk for an individual is low.

For children, their suicide risk factors are a little different to adults because of their age but there is some overlap too. For example, certain factors like age, family dynamics, peer relationships, mental health and gender may increase the risk of suicide.

That's why it's critical for teachers, parents and other adult authority figures to keep this in the back of their mind just in case they need this information. Especially if the warning signs show up.

For all of us, it is not always easy to answer as to why a child or teenager has suicidal thoughts. There are some risk factors like being bullied, neglected, experiencing sexual or physical abuse or other trauma that help to explain it.

Some of the reasons include feeling lonely or socially isolated as well as struggling with a mental health condition. Like depression, bipolar, ADHD or anxiety.

In terms of looking beyond mental health conditions, significant feelings of stress, anger, sadness, or self-doubt and feeling as if they have no one to turn to all increased the risk of suicide.

Additionally, if a child or teenager has lost a loved one, this is a factor that could heighten the risk, and the same goes for a child with recently divorced parents or if their families are facing serious financial trouble.

Furthermore, if there is a lot of family conflict then research shows this is a greater risk factor for young children. But once the child reaches their teen years, conflict with their peers begin to have a more significant effect on mental health than it used to.

And as we looked at in the last chapter, if the teenage or tweens identify themselves as a sexual or gender minority or they're questioning their sexual orientation then this does heightened risk for suicidal ideation. Not because of the identification itself but because of all the societal nonsense surrounding it, like homosexuality is abnormal and they're abominations, and this is all before we consider these risk factors may be exacerbated by being bullied or feeling unsupported by their social support network.

Sadly if we turn our attention to young children for a moment, it is more common for this younger age group to take their lives impulsively, this of course happens in other age groups, but it is more common for young children. This is because they may not know how to cope with difficult feelings and their brains aren't yet developed enough to properly manage their impulses.

In the grand scheme of things, suicide of young children is rare, and limiting access to lethal means can significantly reduce the risk of a child harming themselves suddenly.

And personally I was not going to include this in the book but all the research articles and blog posts and more that I researched for this book kept coming back to locking up guns, handguns and semi-automatic weapons.

Personally, I don't care what you believe or what your stance on gun control is, but as a person who lives in the United Kingdom, everyone (or a very good chunk of people) having a gun is just a strange concept that I flat out don't understand.

But in the interest of trying to unofficially keep as many people safe as possible, LOCK UP YOUR GUNS. It is not hard to lock them up and just keep them away from children to keep them safe and if it's harder to get to the guns then it's harder for them to commit suicide.

I've said it. I've probably annoyed a bunch of people, but I'm writing this book to try to save lives. So I really don't care if I've offended your gun beliefs.

LOCK THEM UP AND SAVE LIVES!

Teenage Suicides:

All the research for the next three paragraphs is from a CDC report published in 2020, if you want to see it all please check out the reference section later in the book.

Anyway, it is a lot more common for teenagers to commit suicide than younger children, because 19% of teenagers self-reported they were seriously considering suicide in 2019, and 9% of teenagers reported attempting suicide in the same period.

Now unlike adults, research suggests that teenage girls are more likely to commit suicide, with them being twice as likely as boys.

Additionally, as mentioned earlier, if a teenager identifies as Lesbian, Gay or Bisexual then this sharply increased the risk with nearly 47% of these teenagers reporting they seriously considered suicide in 2019 and 23% reported they attempted it.

However, this suicide and gender link amongst teenage suicides gets a little stranger for researchers, because research has consistently shown that girls are more likely to attempt suicide than boys, but it is the boys who are more likely to die.

Leading researchers to call this the so-called "suicide gender paradox". This is often attributed to boys' greater propensity to choose more lethal means. Whereas girls tend to use less violent means where their chances of survival are greater.

On the other hand, there is some recent evidence suggesting that the gender gap could be narrowing, at least amongst teenagers, because the suicide rates of teenage girls are higher than in the past. The reason behind this increase appears to be driven by a shift to more lethal means by girls.

Although, it has to be mentioned again like different experts emphasise, regardless of a person's gender, their suicide ideations and thoughts should be taken seriously and responded to rapidly.

You only need to look at the rest of the book to find out how deadly it is when these thoughts are ignored.

Social Media

I definitely feel like some people would be a little disappointed if I didn't mention social media at least once in this book. Then again, there will be readers who, at no fault of their own, believe that social media is absolutely evil when it comes to suicide. And my response to that is a very typical response that most lecturers give students.

Yes. Maybe. No. It depends.

I say this because social media isn't always

bad and it does actually have a lot of benefits for youth. For instance, it improves communication, helps them to develop new interests and it broadens social networks. The problem is when they start to substitute online for real-world connections and activities.

As seen as in a 2017 study from the Royal Society of Public Health and Young Health Movement, in their study they examined 506,820 young people that were aged 13 to 18, and found that adolescents who spent more time on screens had a significantly higher likelihood of experiencing depressive symptoms or having at least one suicide-related outcome.

And the overarching point of the study was that balance is absolutely critical. Since the study found teenagers using electronic devices three or more hours a day had a 34% higher chance of at least 1 suicide-related outcome than those using devices two or less hours a day. As well as adolescents who visited social media sites every day were 13% more likely to report high levels of depressive symptoms.

Moreover, according to research, the popularity measures done by social media companies contribute to depression, because these may lead to feelings of inadequacy when young people see their "friends" having a good time.

Although, this isn't true for all users because if a teenager is well-adjusted, the effect may be the opposite, and it boosts their positive feelings about themselves.

Warning signs:

This is definitely one of the most important sections of the chapter because now we know that child suicide is very real, what are the warning signs to watch out for?

As we saw earlier in the book, there are a lot of warning signs in adults and thankfully the external signs of suicidal ideation in children are similar to the ones that adults might display. But this may vary depending on the child's age, personality and maturity level.

So here are some of the warning signs.

Firstly, changes in behaviours are a sign. For example, if a child suddenly finds it difficult at school, if they withdraw from normal activities, hobbies and friends (like depressed people do) then they become suddenly isolated. As well as their recklessness or impulsivity might increase. In older children and teenagers, their reckless behaviour may include substance use, dangerous driving or sexual promiscuity.

Secondly, if a child excessively talks about dying, self-harm or "going away". Now this is a slightly more tricky one because no one shouldn't panic whenever a child brings up death because of course they're going to be curious about this topic. But the danger comes if there is a large focus on it because this could indicate a deeper issue or difficulty. As well as it is important to remember that children, and this is even more so for young children, don't always have words to express that they want to hurt themselves.

Thirdly, changes in a child's mood is a warning sign. For example, if they're appearing excessively sad, anxious, rageful, restless and irritable. All these could be signals that a child struggling with severe mental health or emotional challenges.

In addition, if they have changes in their appetite, sleep patterns or energy levels. These could be a sign of a medical problem so this isn't too dangerous by itself but is when this is combined with other warning signs that this could be indicative of suicidal thoughts or other mental health difficulties.

Overall, the entire point of talking about warning signs is to highlight that many children and adults tip off their caregiver or other loved ones some way about their intentions. They may do it directly but saying something like *I want to die*. Or they may do it indirectly. For example, by saying *nothing matters anymore*, they're moody or recklessly behave.

And in another vein of this indirect tipping off, in some cases children or teenagers don't want to overtly signal what they're thinking, because they could be a shamed or concerned about what their parents will think.

That's why it's important for parents to take other warning signs of mental health seriously and not assume a child's low mood is "just a phase". And again, evidence clearly shows that asking a child or an adolescent about it will not put that idea in their head, if it wasn't already there.

Additionally, and I need to make sure everyone (including me) remembers this, but in the vast majority of cases the children and adolescents want someone to reach out and show them they're loved, supported and more despite the negative pull of their thoughts.

Therefore, stay involved in their academic lives. I'm horrified personally when I hear that parents aren't involved in their child's academic lives, because if they're struggling or need help, how will they know?

And if a parent's kids are still in school then make sure to attend events that are relevant to them. Such as dance performances and sports matches, as well as if there are any academic problems talk to teachers and faculty.

This is all about showing children and adolescents that they aren't alone and that they are so loved and supported.

And if you ever need to talk to your kid about your suspicions, avoid the idea of having "right or wrong" comments and sure the child knows there are no right answers. Instead try to ask open-ended questions (those that are not answered by a simple yes or no), and this will help them open up to you.

Suicide, Young People And University

Moving onto the final section about university, or college as different parts of the world call it, and how this affects young people.

Therefore, when young people are in college, we know this puts a lot of strain on their mental health and we've all heard about the number of university students that commit suicide, so I won't rehash the findings there.

However, when a young person, loved one or friend goes to university, which tends to be outside of their home state, home town or home-whatever, make sure you keep in touch. Let them know how much you're there for them.

Will they get annoyed at you checking in on them maybe once, twice a week?

Maybe they'll say it, and they will say it if you do it *too frequently*. But they won't truly mean it, and it is always better to be slightly annoying with your love, then not, and find out how badly a person you love is struggling so badly with mental health.

This is even more important for freshmen to Americans, first years to the rest of the world, because many of these students are going through many adaptations, so they need to feel that their family support is still there.

Also when you're calling or seeing them to

check up on them and how they are, make sure you actually listen. Due to instead of them seeking advice, what many young people need is to be heard. Since young people usually make it clear when they want your objective guidance. So a good approach here is to relate their problems to similar ones that you have had in the past.

And this is a lot better and definitely less intrusive than saying things like, *"I think you should."* If they wanted to hear things like that then they would have asked it differently and telling them what you think they should do isn't exactly the perfect support they probably want.

Instead try to give them the space to figure out what is best for them, discuss the different possibilities as well as show them an angle they might not have considered. That's definitely a great way to show them how much you support them.

And because we're nearing the end of a very long but fascinating chapter, please remember that sometimes children and adolescents don't tell you that they're contemplating suicide because they're worried about how you'll react.

As a result, by using direct, non-judgmental questions that are open-ended you can encourage them to share their thoughts and feelings, and regardless of their response, if you suspect that a person might be suicidal, search for professional help immediately.

Overall, finding out someone you loved is naturally very overwhelming and hopefully you won't have to find that out, and you also tend to question they you're a failure of a parent and more. But just remember that these feelings aren't based in reality in the slightest, but they are understandable. As well as parents never have to navigate their emotions alone.

And this is something we haven't really spoke about in the book until now, but whilst your child gets professional help, make sure you get help too. From seeking the support of family members, friends, a therapist or other confidantes, could all help to ensure that the parent is able to care for themselves while ensuring that their child gets the professional help they need.

WHAT IS SUICIDE GRIEF?

After the difficult topic of the last chapter, I really wanted to focus on something slightly different in this next chapter. So we're going to be focusing on the grief experienced by people who have lost loved ones due to suicide.

This chapter sort of serves two purposes in a way. Firstly, it helps us all to understand what these people sadly have to go through and it offers some unofficial guidance to them. Secondly, in case this has happened to you, this chapter offers some perspective that might help you and it helps you to know that you aren't alone.

Therefore, the death of a loved one, even more so when it comes to suicide has a significant impact on every aspect of their life, from their daily functioning to the home life to work life. They are most likely to have intense feelings of sadness, guilt, confusion, anger and grief.

Of course, there is absolutely no right way for suicide survivors to grieve or process their feelings or how they feel about everything.

Especially when they have to do a lot of things they never ever thought they would have to. For instance, having to bury their loved ones, take care of finances and the assets the suicide victim left behind and they are struggling with unanswered questions a lot. All of this takes a massive immense toll on the grieving process.

They have to deal with unanswered questions like:

- Why did they do it?
- Is it my fault?
- Were there warning signs I missed?
- How long was my loved one suffering?
- Could I have prevented this?

All I can say here is as we've seen throughout the book, no it wasn't their fault in the slightest, and there's nothing you could have done.

One of the purposes of this book is to teach and help people become more aware of the signs of suicide for the future. But if you don't know this stuff, you simply don't know. No one talks about this so there's no way you could have known the warning signs or done anything.

This isn't your fault.

In addition, when a suicide survivor engages in emotional numbness, this is a very unhealthy coping mechanism done by their mind to avoid the overwhelming and intense emotions like grief. When they engage in emotional numbness and become emotionally numb, they lose the ability to feel and experience their emotions psychologically and emotionally.

This is often done in clinical terms in connection with dissociation and disconnecting from a person's environment, body, feelings, memories and identity.

Suicide survivors feel like their life is upside down, they're struggling to grasp their new reality without their loved one and they are most likely to blame as well as question themselves.

However, it is so critical, as many therapists encourage, that suicide survivors do actually grieve in their own way and seriously process what they're feeling, or their mental health will only get worse over time.

Furthermore, grief from suicide comes in intense waves and it can come with unexpected emotions during the most unpredicted times.

Nevertheless, it is just essential to be patient and kind to yourself and make sure you allow yourself to feel an emotion as it washes through you then it passes.

Then make sure you also embrace the short moments of peace and joy in-between.

Also, don't let your loved one's suicide define them, because it doesn't. Focus on their achievements and they most probably had an incredible life filled with meaning, focus on that joy and celebrate their life.

Moreover, find suicide support groups, because there are so many people like you that are willing to share their own experiences and even if you don't feel ready to share your own just yet, just listen. And know you aren't alone and it will help you to feel less isolated.

Another piece of unofficial advice is to keep a journal because research shows that writing can be a therapeutic way to work through the dark side of grief.

Of course, you will need to be prepared for painful reminders of your loss. For example, holidays you might have booked together but aren't able to go on now, or family holidays like Christmas or whatever else you celebrate. Then there are birthdays and anniversaries as well. In this most impossible of moments, try to celebrate them in honour of your loved one or create new memories on these days by starting new traditions.

In addition, you will have to expect to have ups and downs in the future, so you need to brace yourself for these powerful emotions because you will have some bad days and some good days. Lean into both of them and allow yourself to sit with emotions until they pass.

However, one of the most important things in this entire chapter is you have to allow yourself to find joy. I know many survivors feel guilty about experiencing happiness, but you have to allow yourself to feel joy, to laugh and to have fun. Laughter and joy are not signs of "less grief". Instead they are part of the grieving process and of course your loved one would want you to experience happy moments.

Overall, when you're faced with grief, allow these feelings to flow through you, speak about your grief so it doesn't build up, allow yourself to express your feelings and focus on moving away from the feelings of dying and death towards a focus that promotes life and living.

This entire process and course of both good and bad emotions is normal, okay and part of the grieving process. You can still remember and celebrate your amazing loved one, and still live a purposeful as well as fulfilling life that is not primarily led or ruled by grief.

NEUROPSYCHOLOGY OF SUICIDE

After focusing so much on the social and cognitive factors in the form of mental health conditions that impact people's suicide risk, we now need to really change it up and focus on the biological side of suicide in the form of neuropsychology.

In other words, how does the brain impact a person's chances of committing suicide?

The main reason we're looking at this area is because I truly want to give us all the most information as possible about suicide, and that involves looking at every area possible. Resulting in us now moving onto the brain.

Therefore, to investigate how the brain affects suicide Schmaal et al. (2020) decided to investigate what brain areas were involved in suicidal decision-making, and their results showed that it was the brain areas and systems related to emotion and impulse regulation.

For example, the Ventral Pre-Frontal Cortex (VPFC) was one of the areas involved with increased suicide risk being associated with impairments in middle as well as side regions of the VPFC, and impairments to the brain connections in this cortex appearing to play a role in excessive negative and blunted positive internal states that can stimulate suicidal ideation.

Additionally, the impairments in the Dorsal Prefrontal Cortex (DPFC) and its connections with the inferior frontal gyrus are associated with suicide attempt behaviours.

Moreover, both the VPFC and DPFC are connected to a portion of the Dorsal Anterior Cingulate Cortez (dACC) and insula. These two brain regions might mediate the transition from suicidal thoughts (as in thinking about suicide) to behaviours (preparing and planning to carry it out and then the suicide itself) by switching between VPFC and DPFC brain systems.

If we connect this information to the other areas of the book, we know from studies like Yeh et al. (2019) that there is a high risk of suicidality amongst clients with depressive disorders, bipolar disorder and schizophrenia spectrum disorders. But if we connect this to neuropsychology then it's interesting to know that these conditions are associated with alterations in the VPFC, insula, dACC and DPFC.

On the whole, there is hope within the neuroscience and psychology communities that if we understand the neurocircuitry well enough in relation to suicide. Then we can hopefully create more effective and targeted interventions and develop more preventive measures.

Before I give a closing remark in this shorter chapter, I want to mention and slightly remind the need for a holistic approach here, because as always it is all well and good us focusing on brain areas, and "fixing" the brain areas to prevent suicide. But it is useless if the person still has social and cognitive factors that make them suicidal.

For example, if they have an unhealthy family dynamic that makes them want to commit suicide, or if they have a negative cognitive style that again makes them see suicide as they only escape, "fixing" brain areas will only go so far.

Therefore, yes we need the neuropsychological interventions for these brain areas but we mustn't forget the importance of psychological treatments too, and even drug interventions if they are absolutely necessary.

But even if that doesn't come completely true, it still connects with what we looked at in chapter two of the book. Due to at the very least all this research proves that there is something more going on behind the cause of suicidal thoughts and behaviours than so-called cowardice, weakness or any number of mistakenly labelled character flaws attributed to those that commit suicide.

WHAT LINKS PERSONALITY AND SUICIDE?

Moving onto personality psychology factors, I want to give you a mini-crash course as a little introduction to personality psychology in case you aren't familiar with it.

The focus of this chapter will be the Big Five Factor Model which divides personality traits into five large categories or factors, and to help you understand this better, below is the extract from my Personality Psychology And Individual Differences book:

"As a result, the Big Five personality factors are:

- Neuroticism
- Extroversion
- Openness to Experience
- Agreeableness
- Conscientiousness

Now, we'll look at these personality factors and all of the information here comes from Pervin et al (2005).

Neuroticism:

This first personality factor assesses a person's maladjustment vs emotional stability. Meaning it finds out if people are prone to unrealistic ideas, psychological distress and excessive cravings or urges. As well as if they have any maladaptive coping responses.

Extroversion

I think we can all agree with has to be the most famous personality factor because of its popularity in media, TV and books. And you can easily see this trait in everyday life.

In addition, this Big factor assesses the quantity and intensity of a person's capacity of joy, interpersonal relationships, activity level and need for simulation.

Since an extrovert has a high activity level with a lot of need for stimulation whereas an introvert is the opposite.

Openness to Experience

This I think has to be one of the most interesting as it looks at a person's behaviour towards proactively seeking out as well as appreciating an experience for their own sake. And it assesses a person's tolerance for exploring the unfamiliar.

Personally, I do like this personality dimension as I think I'm rather high in it because I love exploring new places, the woods and local areas. But to some extent, I don't really like leaving my comfort zone too often depending on the situation.

Agreeableness

Despite the name suggesting you agree with everyone if you're high in this dimension. Agreeableness looks at how kind, gentle and sympathetic a person is.

Conscientiousness:

The last dimension assesses an individual's degree of organisation, persistence and motivation in goal directed behaviour. As well as it contrasts people who are dependable and organised with people who are lackadaisical and sloppy."

Personality and Suicide:

Now we know the basics of personality psychology, the Big Five factor model has been found to predict a wide range of important life outcomes. For instance, after general intelligence, conscientiousness is the single best predictor of a person's work or academic performance.

Also, as you'll see in the next chapter, it has long been known that personality disorders, like Borderline Personality Disorder, are associated with higher risk of suicide. Yet it is less well known that 5% of Antisocial Personality Disorder will eventually die by suicide.

For the next part of the chapter, we're going to be looking at a range of research behind personality factors and suicide, then I'll explain the implications of the results at the end.

Firstly, Ansell et al. (2015) investigated 431 patients with personality disorders for 10 years, and over that time 13.5% of the patients made at least one or more suicide attempts with the maximum being 11. Therefore, showing that people with personality disorders are at a higher risk of suicide compared to the general population.

Secondly, other researchers wanted to investigate the relationship between a person's suicide risk and the five-factor personality traits. For instance, Duberstein et al. (2000) examined 81 depressed inpatients who were aged 50 or over, and the researchers found they had higher levels of neuroticism and openness to experience. Both of these were associated with having a history of suicidal ideation, whereas lower levels of extraversion was associated with having a history of past suicide attempts.

Thirdly, within the same research vein as Duberstein, McCann (2010) looked at the relationship of personality at a State level in the US (for example people in Nebraska are less neurotic than people in New Jersey) and compared it to the state's suicide completion rates. The results showed that higher neuroticism rates in states and lower levels of agreeableness increased rates of death by suicide. Those two personality traits combined accounted for approximately half of the variance in suicide rates amongst all 50 states.

Then if we move onto studies that had much larger sample sizes, Bluml et al. (2013) looked at 2,555 German citizens and assessed their Big Five personality traits and suicide risk. Bluml's results found significant differences between men and women. Such as female suicide risk was increased when neuroticism was higher and when openness to experience was higher. Whereas male suicide risk decreased in the presence of higher extroversion and higher conscientiousness.

I'll talk about the results in a moment.

For our penultimate study, Soltaninejad et al. (2014) studied 1,659 members of the Iranian armed forces. This is great on its own because it allows the literature to have a wide range of findings from different countries and cultures to inform their results, so we can predict or suggest a universal rule of behaviour which personality factors for suicide seems to be.

Therefore, their results found neuroticism was a stronger predictor of current suicidal thinking, then extroversion was the second, and then agreeableness was the third. Meaning that higher levels of neuroticism, lower extroversion and agreeableness increased risk of suicidal ideation in this sample.

Finally, the largest study that I could find was Batty et al. (2018) who monitored 464,251 participants in several countries over a period of 8 years. During this time 270 participants died by suicide, and the results found higher levels of neuroticism significantly increased suicide risk and lower levels of agreeableness contributed to higher risk as well but less dramatically.

Discussion Of Results

In terms of the results, some researchers have dubbed these findings as the "Misery Triad". Due to the combination of these traits suggests the person has a greater sensitivity to emotional pain, they lack effectiveness in solving their difficulties and resisting impulses and a deficiency of social support. Also, studies that implicated lower agreeableness added to "lack of social support increases suicide risk" hypothesis.

Overall, neuroticism is clearly a strong factor when it comes to suicide risk and it should be corrected by psychotherapy that this teaches the person how to better manage negative emotions and in some cases psychiatric medication might be appropriate too in the intervention.

For the lower conscientiousness risk factor, this is a risk factor because these people are more impulsive and might be more at risk of making poorly considered decisions to attempt suicide. As well as it is associated with worse performance in school and at work. This is very important to remember as a third of successful suicides are unemployed at time of death.

But one personality trait that does need more research into is the openness to experience, because suicide isn't the sort of open experience that people should want to experience, and this is a surprising finding that researchers don't understand.

Yet.

OTHER MENTAL HEALTH CONDITIONS AND SUICIDE

To sort of start wrapping up the book, these final two chapters are going to be picking up on details that we might have missed in other chapters. For example, in this chapter because we have already spoken about depression and bipolar disorder a lot in the book, we now need to focus on some other mental health conditions to see how they impact suicide.

Suicide Amongst Post-Traumatic Stress Disorder

The first condition we'll look at is PTSD and this develops in the aftermath of a traumatic event, with it being a complex condition that manifests in several different ways. Including, depression, dissociation and anxiety. Leading PTSD to reduce a person's quality of life and it is sometimes implicated in suicide.

Additionally, according to a September 2018 VA report, the veterans overall suicide rate is approximately 1.5 times higher than non-veterans, with male veterans more likely than females.

Saying that, in the last few years, suicides amongst female veterans have been rapidly increasing with recent evidence suggesting female veterans are more likely by two to five times to die by suicide compared to non-veteran females.

Overall, if someone has PTSD then it is critical that they seek professional help for the condition. Not only so they can improve their quality of life, but so they can also prevent possible suicide down the line.

Borderline Personality Disorder

The second condition we'll be looking at is Borderline Personality Disorder with it being characterised by a person's unstable moods, intense fear of abandonment as well as difficulty in maintaining personal relationships.

In terms of suicide, this is an important condition to look at because approximately 70% of people with Borderline Personality Disorder will attempt suicide, 10% will die by it.

The treatment for the condition is typically a form of psychotherapy, like Dialectical behavioural therapy, that is combined with medication, leaving people able to be stabilised and live fulfilling productive lives.

Moreover, if we cast our minds back to the second chapter of the book on myths and the reference to *suicide as attention seeking,* this is slightly possible with Borderline Personality Disorder as threats of suicide or self-harm are a common symptom of BPD especially in response to perceived rejection or abandonment by friends, loved ones or romantic partners. Yet it is still important that threats are be taken seriously as many people BPD do attempt it.

On the other hand, these threats of suicide do create intense emotional strain or frustration for the people on the receiving end, even more when it occurs often over a long period of time, so anyone who thinks a loved one at risk should help immediately.

I'll fully admit this is a trickier condition to work with because the use of suicide threats is common, but considering how many BPD sufferers do attempt suicide, getting professional help is still just as critical as it is for any other case.

Substance Abuse and Suicide

The penultimate condition we need to focus on is substance abuse and this is a very important one to look at because it of how common it is. Especially with substance abusers being approximately 6 times more likely to die by suicide than the general population.

Also it's good to note that many people with addiction who consider suicide do struggle with depression or another mental health condition. This only increases the risk of suicide anyway.

Therefore, the best way to avoid a suicide is to treat the addiction and any other concurrent condition at the same time to decrease the risk of suicide and help the person better cope with negative emotions in the future.

As well as one of the reasons why substance abuse is a flawed maladaptive coping mechanism is because drug use itself can trigger depressive states or low mood, as seen in "downer" drugs like alcohol or sedatives. Then other kinds of drugs lower inhibitions, leading people to behave impulsively or take dangerous actions they wouldn't take while sober.

And referring to the coping mechanism, drug use could attempt to cope with negative emotions, it actually may help suppress bad feelings in the short term. But that's the thing about the short term, it's short and drugs tends to worsen a person's emotional state over time, and when drugs run out and painful emotions come back, the person could feel overwhelmed by sadness and consider suicide a way out.

Attention-Deficit Hyperactivity Disorder, Autism and Suicide

In the stages of writing this book, there was actually going to be a chapter dedicated to this condition because I found a rather interesting looking article that I was going to save for later. Yet when I came back to the article, I realised the single research study mentioned in it was far too tedious for my liking, so I ditched the idea.

Thankfully, I managed to find a new study that helps to examine how ADHD and suicide interconnect in the form of Furczyk et al. (2014) and a few others in the reference section at the end of the book.

The study shows that ADHD appears to cause a noticeable increased risk of suicide, because people with the condition struggle with impulsivity, so they could be more likely to engage in self-harming behaviour or consider suicide when faced with a career setback, low mood or relationship upset.

Furthermore, impulsive people are more likely to take part in substance abuse. This as we saw in the last section can increase the risk of suicide.

Also, the symptoms of inattention may lead to the person experiencing social, career or academic-related challenges which results in damage to their self-esteem, as well as persistently low self-esteem or feelings that they're a failure can trigger or worsen suicidal ideation.

Additionally, ADHD and depression frequently appear side by side and this further heightens the risk of suicidal thoughts or behaviour.

Similarly, evidence from Hirvikoski et al. (2020) suggests that people with Autism Spectrum Conditions are significantly more likely to attempt suicide than the general population, with them being approximately 4 to 6 times more likely. The risk appears to be even greater for women with autism and that is probably linked to the diagnostic and support problems engrained in ASC towards women, but that's beyond the scope of this book.

As well as people who also have ADHD or have ADHD and an intellectual disability are maybe at an even greater risk according to Hirvikoski et al. (2020).

Overall, the data suggests clinicians should be especially vigilant for signs of suicidality in individuals with autism and experts argue particularly if other risk factors are present.

And to finish up this mental health section of the book, I just wanted to jump in here and remind us of all, including myself, that yes having a mental health condition does affect a person's quality of life, causes psychological distress and results in maladaptive coping mechanisms that need to be effectively trained out of a person.

It does not mean they are "fated" (if you believe in that stuff) to commit suicide or attempt it.

I know a lot of the book has focused on mental health conditions and how they impact suicide, but the former does not guarantee the latter.

My point is if you know someone who has a mental health condition that we're spoken about in the book, please don't panic that they're "doomed" to attempt suicide. They aren't.

Just love them, support them and if they show a warning sign or you're concerned about them, then take action and make sure they know how much you value them.

OTHER SUICIDE RISK FACTORS

For the final chapter of the book, I know we've covered a lot of suicide risk factors and why people might unfortunately choose suicide as the only way to stop the pain. But suicide isn't always down or caused by mental health conditions, substance abuse or any other conditions.

Instead, the person's choice could be down to one or more wide ranging sociocultural or physical factors. For example, chronic pain, job loss, unemployment or serious legal trouble (as we saw in the prison chapter) and genetics. As well as I'm sure you've noticed through the book, but suicide is a very complicated matter.

Therefore, there are a few more causes or risk factors we need to look at together before we finish up our psychology journey.

Economic And Social Challenges:

As social and other fields of psychology teaches us, as a species as humans do not exist in a vacuum. We are constantly influenced by external and internal factors from our social groups to our biology to our society.

As humans, we are very, very dependent on other people and communities for resources, social contact, food and nourishment (sustenance) and endless other needs.

As a result, when these connections are severed for whatever reason, the effect of this is very severe, and sometimes drive others to suicide.

In terms of economic factors, if someone has lost their job then this creates significant financial challenges for them that are hard to overcome. The social and economic factors themselves worsen a person's risk of suicide, but being evicted and unable to pay rent is strongly associated with increased risk of suicidal thoughts and behaviours.

Additionally, there is evidence that 1 in 3 people who died by suicide were unemployed at the time. As well as during economic downturns, there's an increase in suicide rates. For example, evidence from the 2008 recession showed that there was an associated 13% increase in suicides, with many of these being attributed to unemployment.

In terms of genetics and I realise this is a bit off the cuff, but because mental health conditions have a genetic component and the certain conditions themselves can increase the risk of suicide. There's an argument too that genetics are a suicide risk factor, but of course it is a lot more complicated than that.

That's why it's a bit off the cuff without me going into too much depth.

How Chronic Pain Links With Suicide?

This was definitely a bit of a surprise for me to learn about because I never would have considered this a risk factor, but of course now I know about it, it makes perfect sense.

Chronic pain increases the risk of suicide too because evidence suggests that chronic pain sufferers are twice as likely to consider suicide. This is even more true if they suffer long term severe pain, and this can significantly interfere with a person's ability to work, take care of themselves and provide for a family.

Resulting in feelings of inadequacy, it can strain their relationships and put financial challenges on them, and then to make this even worse this is combined with the daily agony of the pain itself. Leading to significantly worsen a person's mental health over a period of months or years.

This is absolutely terrible, but sadly the bad news doesn't always stop here.

Since if the cause of the chronic pain is unclear or their treatment is ineffective, then this can and does lead to feelings of hopelessness. And that same happens if a person's chronic pain is dismissed or ignored by doctors. All resulting in a person's well-being being damaged further, and suicide being seen as the only way out.

And even some of the medication given to people with chronic pain isn't great, because opioid medication is frequently prescribed to treat chronic pain. But it can lead to mental or physical dependence on the drug so when the medication runs out or is otherwise no longer available, the withdrawal symptoms can heighten their feelings of despair.

Thankfully, there are things that can be done about chronic pain and decrease the suicidal feelings. Like having effective medical treatment reduces or eliminates chronic pain, leading to a significantly lower suicide risk.

Equally, if the biological treatments are imperfect then psychological treatments, like mindfulness-based stress based or Cognitive Behavioural Therapy or lifestyle changes promoting a healthier diet, better sleep and physical activity can all help build up a person's self-efficacy, as well as target their rumination and anxiety that are inherent to chronic pain.

Overall, with their mental health improving because of the effective treatment, and they no longer have the rumination as well as the anxiety surrounding their chronic pain, this all leads to a reduction of the intensity and frequency of their suicidal behaviours and thoughts.

And that's a great result for anyone.

CONCLUSION

After looking at the causes, risk factors, how to prevent suicide and more, we need to wrap up everything, and this is definitely easier said than done. Simply because we have looked at so much, so instead I will just give some unofficial pointers and tips for all of us moving forward.

Thankfully, many of us will never have to deal with suicide directly, and for the people who picked up this book because they were curious about learning more about suicide. It is great that you have wanted to learn more and now you know that there are so many myths and harming misconceptions about suicide, and now all of us know what actually happens.

Therefore, to these people, I, of course, thank you massively for picking up this book, and I think going forward we just need to challenge people when they repeat the false damaging myths that only harm suicidal individuals instead of helping them.

Because let's face it, these myths kill people. These myths stop people from feeling able to reach out and get support, so these myths need to end. And that can all start with us challenging them whenever we face them.

For the people who have faced loss by suicide and you picked up this book, I know you will probably be in the minority of the readers. But I really hope I gave you something useful. Maybe I helped you understand what happened, maybe I helped you understand that it wasn't your fault and maybe I helped give you a little bit of closure.

And like all readers of my books, it's been a privilege that you picked up my book on the topic.

Just remember that no suicide is your fault and now we all know about the warning signs, the causes and the research about suicide. We can all watch our loved ones just in case this happens, because it is always better to know than not know, and then something bad happens.

Finally, I have no idea if anyone who is thinking about suicide would read a book like this, but just in case they are. Please just get professional help, talk to someone and just know that you are loved, supported and cherished by your loved ones.

You might be feeling alone right now and like you are an awful burden on the entire world. I know that, truly. But things do get so much better and you really are loved.

We have explored in the book how to tell others about your feelings, the importance of hotlines and what to do if you cannot talk to your loved ones. But seek help, you aren't worthless and the world does need you, no matter what your thoughts tell you otherwise.

I truly hope that everyone has gotten something out of this book. Personally I loved writing it and I truly hope that this helps to make a difference to someone's life.

I doubt I will, I really do, but I had to try.

REFERENCE LIST

Alcaide, J., Guirado, R., Crespo, C. et al. (2019). Alterations of perineuronal nets in the dorsolateral prefrontal cortex of neuropsychiatric patients. Int. J. Bipolar Disord., 7:24. doi.org/10.1186/s40345-019-0161-0

Ansell, E. B., Wright, A. G., Markowitz, J. C., Sanislow, C. A., Hopwood, C. J., Zanarini, M. C., ... & Grilo, C. M. (2015). Personality disorder risk factors for suicide attempts over 10 years of follow-up. *Personality Disorders: Theory, Research, and Treatment*, *6*(2), 161.

Asarnow JR & Mehlum L. (2019). Practitioner Review: Treatment for suicidal and self-harming adolescents - advances in suicide prevention care. Journal of child psychology and psychiatry, and allied disciplines, 60(10), 1046–1054. https://doi.org/10.1111/jcpp.13130

Batty, G. D., Gale, C. R., Tanji, F., Gunnell, D., Kivimäki, M., Tsuji, I., & Jokela, M. (2018). Personality traits and risk of suicide mortality: findings from a multi-cohort study in the general population. *World psychiatry : official journal of the World Psychiatric Association (WPA)*, *17*(3), 371–372. https://doi.org/10.1002/wps.20575

Bouras C., Kövari E., Hof P.R., et al. (2001). Anterior cingulate cortex pathology in schizophrenia and bipolar disorder. Acta Neuropathol., 102(4):373-9. 10.1007/s004010100392

Bridge, J. A., Asti, L., Horowitz, L. M., Greenhouse, J. B., Fontanella, C. A., Sheftall, A. H., ... & Campo, J. V. (2015). Suicide trends among elementary school–aged children in the United States from 1993 to 2012. *JAMA pediatrics*, *169*(7), 673-677.

Curtin, S. C., & Heron, M. P. (2019). Death rates due to suicide and homicide among persons aged 10–24: United States, 2000–2017.

Duberstein, P. R., Conwell, Y., Seidlitz, L., Denning, D. G., Cox, C., & Caine, E. D. (2000). Personality traits and suicidal behavior and ideation in depressed inpatients 50 years of age and older. *The journals of gerontology. Series B, Psychological sciences and social sciences*, *55*(1), P18–P26. https://doi.org/10.1093/geronb/55.1.p18

Duncan, D.T. and Hatzenbuehler, M.L., 2014. Lesbian, gay, bisexual, and transgender hate crimes and suicidality among a population-based sample of sexual-minority adolescents in Boston. American journal of public health, 104(2), pp.272-278.

Furczyk K & Thome J. (2014). Adult ADHD and suicide. Atten Defic Hyperact Disord. 6(3):153-8.

Gunnell D, Appleby L, Arensman E, et al. (2020). Suicide risk and prevention during the COVID-19 pandemic. Lancet Psychiatry. 7(6):468-471. doi:10.1016/S2215-0366(20)30171-1

Hirvikoski, T., Boman, M., Chen, Q., D'Onofrio, B., Mittendorfer-Rutz, E., Lichtenstein, P., . . . Larsson, H. (n.d.). (2020) Individual risk and familial liability for suicide attempt and suicide in autism: A population-based study. Psychological Medicine, 1-12.

doi:10.1017/S0033291719001405

https://archive.nytimes.com/newoldage.blogs.nytimes.com/2013/08/07/high-suicide-rates-among-the-elderly

https://www.canada.ca/en/public-health/services/publications/healthy-living/suicide-canada-key-statistics-infographic.html

https://www.nimh.nih.gov/health/statistics/suicide

https://www.psychologytoday.com/gb/basics/depression/depression-and-suicide

https://www.psychologytoday.com/gb/basics/suicide/how-talk-about-suicidal-thoughts

https://www.psychologytoday.com/gb/basics/suicide/warning-signs-suicide

https://www.psychologytoday.com/gb/blog/cell-block/201902/suicide-behind-bars

https://www.psychologytoday.com/gb/blog/happiness-is-state-mind/202109/suicide-prevention-awareness-month-what-is-suicide-grief

https://www.psychologytoday.com/gb/blog/reading-between-the-headlines/201412/suicide-and-the-holidays

https://www.psychologytoday.com/us/blog/happiness-is-state-mind/202005/mental-health-and-job-loss

https://www.psychologytoday.com/us/blog/nation-in-pain/201511/chronic-pain-and-the-risk-suicide

https://www.psychologytoday.com/us/blog/talking-about-men/202109/the-silent-crisis-male-suicide

https://www.psychologytoday.com/us/blog/talking-about-men/202109/the-silent-crisis-male-suicide

https://www.spectrumnews.org/news/autistic-women-twice-as-likely-as-autistic-men-to-attempt-suicide/

Impey M & Heun R. (2012) Completed suicide, ideation and attempt in attention deficit hyperactivity disorder. Acta Psychiatr Scand. 125(2):93-102.

Isumi A, Doi S, Yamaoka Y, Takahashi K, Fujiwara T. (2020). Do suicide rates in children and adolescents change during school closure in Japan? The acute effect of the first wave of COVID-19 pandemic on child and adolescent mental health [published online ahead of print, 2020 Aug 23]. Child Abuse Negl. doi:10.1016/j.chiabu.2020.104680

Ivey-Stephenson, A. Z., Demissie, Z., Crosby, A. E., Stone, D. M., Gaylor, E., Wilkins, N., ... & Brown, M. (2020). Suicidal ideation and behaviors among high school students—youth risk behavior survey, United States, 2019. *MMWR supplements*, *69*(1), 47.

Janiri, D., Doucet, G. E., Pompili, M., Sani, G., Luna, B., Brent, D. A., & Frangou, S. (2020). Risk and protective factors for childhood suicidality: a US population-based study. *The Lancet Psychiatry*, *7*(4), 317-326.

Killgore WDS, Cloonan SA, Taylor EC, et al. (2020). Trends in suicidal ideation over the first three months of COVID-19 lockdowns [published online ahead of print, 2020 Aug 17]. Psychiatry Res. 293:113390. doi:10.1016/j.psychres.2020.113390

McCann S. J. (2010). Suicide, big five personality factors, and depression at the American state level. *Archives of suicide research : official journal of the International Academy for Suicide Research*, *14*(4), 368–374. https://doi.org/10.1080/13811118.2010.524070

Namkung, H., Kim, S. H., & Sawa, A. (2017). The Insula: An Underestimated Brain Area in Clinical Neuroscience, Psychiatry, and Neurology. Trends in Neurosciences, 40(4):200–207. https://doi.org/10.1016/j.tins.2017.02.002

Nordentoft M & Erlangsen A. (2019). Suicide-turning the tide. Science (New York, N.Y.), 365(6455), 725. https://doi.org/10.1126/science.aaz1568

Schmaal, L., van Harmelen, A.L., Chatzi, V. et al. (2020). Imaging suicidal thoughts and behaviors: a comprehensive review of 2 decades of neuroimaging studies. Mol. Psychiatry, 25:408–427. doi.org/10.1038/s41380-019-0587-x

Soltaninejad, A., Fathi-Ashtiani, A., Ahmadi, K., Mirsharafoddini, H. S., Nikmorad, A., & Pilevarzadeh, M. (2014). Personality factors underlying suicidal behavior among military youth. *Iranian Red Crescent medical journal*, *16*(4), e12686. https://doi.org/10.5812/ircmj.12686

Turecki G & Brent DA (2016). Suicide and suicidal behaviour. The Lancet, 387, 1227–1239.

Twenge JM, Joiner TE. (2020). U.S. Census Bureau-assessed prevalence of anxiety and depressive symptoms in 2019 and during the 2020 COVID-19 pandemic [published online ahead of print, 2020 Jul 15]. Depress Anxiety. 10.1002/da.23077. doi:10.1002/da.23077

Uddin R, Burton NW, Maple M, Khan SR, Khan A. (2019). Suicidal ideation, suicide planning, and suicide attempts among adolescents in 59 low-income and middle-income countries: a population-based study. The Lancet Child & Adolescent Health. 3 (4): 223–233. doi:10.1016/S2352-4642(18)30403-6. PMID 30878117.

VA National Suicide Data Report 2005-2016, Office of Mental Health and Suicide Prevention, September 2018

Womer, F. Y., Kalmar, J. H., Wang, F., & Blumberg, H. P. (2009). A Ventral Prefrontal-Amygdala Neural System in Bipolar Disorder: A View from Neuroimaging Research. Acta Neuropsychiatrica, 21(6):228–238. PMCID: PMC2911239

Yeh, H. H., Westphal, J., Hu, Y. et al. (2019). Diagnosed mental health conditions and risk of suicide mortality. Psychiatric Services, 70(9):750–757. doi: 10.1176/appi.ps.201800346

WRITTEN BY RAPE SURVIVOR
CONNOR WHITELEY
HEALING AS
A SURVIVOR
A PERSONAL AND CLINICAL PSYCHOLOGY GUIDE TO HEALING FROM SEXUAL VIOLENCE

HEALING AS A SURVIVOR

A Personal And Clinical Psychology Guide To Healing From Sexual Violence

INTRODUCTION

This is a book about healing, recovery and thriving after being raped and experiencing sexual violence.

You don't need to have read my past two books on sexual violence to read and enjoy this one. *I Am Not A Victim, I Am A Survivor* is a very personal book that details my mental health, my trauma responses and how I navigated life for the first five months after my rape before my specialist counselling started. This book might provide a lot of context for why I needed this specialist counselling so badly but it is not needed to appreciate this book.

Whereas *Breaking The Silence* is a psychology-focused book on the research, facts and figures of sexual violence so why does it happen, what makes men and women commit sexual violence against others, how can we support survivors and more.

Both books are brilliant additions to this one.

What Does This Book Cover?

Healing As A Survivor is a deeply personal, moving and potentially heartwarming book about my recovery and healing from sexual trauma. It covers each of my specialist counselling sessions, the insights I learnt about myself that allowed me to heal and a lot of useful techniques and concepts that I learnt along the way.

Nothing in this book is any sort of official mental health advice, but I still talk about everything that I found helpful and all the extra things that I was going through as I healed from sexual trauma.

If you want to understand what it's like to recover from PTSD, anxiety, hypervigilance, depression and more trauma responses that sexual violence can cause, then this is a brilliant book for you.

Who Is This Book For?

Mainly, I wrote this book for survivors and for anyone who wants to understand what survivors go through and what it takes to heal. For instance, friends, family and therapists working with survivors of sexual violence.

Survivors might find this insightful, engaging and very relatable book useful because it clearly shows that recovery is possible. It isn't easy, it isn't linear and it can be painful at times, but healing is possible. Also, this book will show that what you're experiencing isn't abnormal, strange or messed-up.

You are trying to deal with an extremely abnormal situation so what is happening to you is normal given the situation.

This book helps to show you how recovery can happen, how counselling works and it demystifies the process for you.

Loved ones and friends could find this book useful too because this book helps to show you what your friends and loved one might be thinking, feeling and experiencing. As well as you can show this engaging and conversational book to the survivor in your life so they know that healing is possible.

In addition, therapists might find this book a useful guide to some of the concepts you might want to explore with clients, and this book will help you gain a deeper understanding of what it takes to recover from sexual violence. This includes the psychoeducational and physical aspects related to the trauma.

Everyone has the potential to find this book interesting, heartbreaking and useful.

Who Am I?

In my other psychology books, I include this section because I like to know who the author is so I know the information is coming from a reliable and good source, but I'm including this section for a different reason.

I'm Connor Whiteley, the internationally bestselling author of over 40 psychology books, I am the host of *The Psychology World Podcast,* a weekly show exploring a new psychology topic each week and delivering the latest psychology news. Available on all major podcast apps and YouTube. As well as I am a psychology graduate who studied a Clinical Psychology undergraduate and Masters at the University of Kent, England.

I am a survivor, not a victim.

I love psychology, spending time with my friends, going out and living. Also, I like fiction books of all types especially books by Dean Wesley Smith, and I like watching films with my friends.

I am a normal person with a normal, fun,

exciting life but when I was raped, he took everything from me.

Originally, I thought I was a weak victim but I am not. I have healed from what he did to me.

I am a survivor, not a victim, but it wasn't always that way.

This is my story of recovery and this is my truth.

MEETING THE THERAPIST, CONTRACTS AND MORE: LESSONS FROM A GREAT FIRST SESSION

This book is going to be an honest account of my therapy sessions starting with my first to my twelfth specialist counselling session designed to support sexual violence survivors to heal and thrive.

Of course I'm not going to pretend that I wasn't nervous, scared and a little numb before my first session. Since if you've read my previous book *I Am Not A Victim, I Am A Survivor,* then you know the month before my rape counselling started, my mental health just died.

I had already been experiencing severe Post-Traumatic Stress Disorder, severe panic attacks, nightmares and on and on and on. My mental health was a mess so I was very nervous about starting counselling because I needed the support more than ever, and a part of me was scared that it wasn't going to work.

I was scared that if my counselling didn't work then I was going to be "messed up" for life and there was no hope that I would be able to survive, heal and thrive from my trauma. Also, I was scared that if that happened then He had won, my rapist had won over me and I would never be able to move on from the messed-up rubbish he did to me that night.

That was why I was scared and nervous about my first counselling session.

In addition, the weirdest thing about it was that even though my mental health was dead in the month of August 2024 and that continued for a while afterwards. I still placed so much hope on getting my rape counselling and I was always waiting for that phone call telling me when my first appointment was.

However, I remember when the call came, it was 10:30 in the morning on the Wednesday before my first session. I was grateful for it and I thanked the lady on the phone, but I felt numb and I couldn't feel anything.

I couldn't *feel* happiness, relief or any sort of emotion whatsoever, and that was odd. It was weird to me that for the past three months, I had been waiting and fighting to be okay enough to have these sessions that I was expecting to feel more when I received them.

I did not. I felt absolutely dead inside.

Therefore, I'm telling you this because I want you to know that it's okay if you react to finding getting professional help in a counterintuitive way. Some people will cry in happiness, some people will feel so hopeful and other people will feel the best they have in months because they've finally got an appointment.

However, it's okay if you don't. After experiencing sexual violence, it's okay if you experience emotions differently to how your brain tells you you should logically feel. If you feel nervous, scared or even concerned about your therapy or counselling. That is okay.

It is just your body and your brain reacting in a normal way to an extremely abnormal situation.

Sexual violence is never ever your fault and there is nothing you could have done to stop or change what happened to you. The fault always lies with whoever did it to you.

You never should have had to go to therapy because your sexual violence experience never should have happened, and that's on your attacker.

It is never on you.

What Happened During My First Session? Meeting The Counsellor

I already mentioned that I was nervous about my first counselling session and thankfully it turned out I had absolutely nothing to be nervous about. Since my counsellor was a really lovely lady, let's call her Kay (a fake name) for the purpose of this book. She was really kind, happy and positive person who happened to be a humanistic counsellor.

In other words, she focuses on you doing a lot of your own healing outside of sessions, and she believes that you already know the answers to your own healing and thriving, sometimes you just need a little support getting to those answers for yourself.

In the next chapter, you'll learn about what Person-Centred Therapy is, because that therapy contains a lot of ideas that humanistic counsellors draw on and use in their work.

Personally, as a clinical psychology Masters student at the time of writing and a survivor, I really like this model. Since it's very client-focused so I know I'm in control, she is working *with* me and never ever against me and it's an empowering model. I have all the answers, I do know myself and I am strong enough to heal. I just need some guidance and help from a counsellor.

That's why I am an empowered survivor, not a victim.

Moreover, I want to mention here that even if you feel like you cannot be an empowered survivor, and only a victim that has connotations of being weak, helpless and broken. I want you to know that I used to think the same, and I talk a lot more about my own experiences of powerlessness and all the mental health consequences of my rape in my book.

Yet I want you to know that as you continue to heal, get professional help and you continue your trauma recovery. You can become empowered and you can stop seeing yourself as a victim.

The Contract, Confidentiality And Explaining Specialist Counselling

Now I have to admit that as a clinical psychology student, I always rather enjoy these first sessions because I know how important they are in developing what's known as the therapeutic alliance. This is essentially the relationship you have with your therapist or counsellor and how good this relationship is can be a powerful predictor in the success of the therapy.

Nonetheless, it's impressive how you need to create a good enough relationship in the space of 50 minutes that the client trusts you enough that they want to come back, and trust you enough that they're willing to open up to you.

Due to it is perfectly acceptable for you not to open up with someone who you don't like or aren't comfortable with. If that is the case then you might need a new counsellor or therapist.

Therefore, when it came to my counsellor, we spoke a little about ourselves so we could get to know each other a little more. As well as this is the ultimate aim of the first session, it is all about establishing that therapeutic relationship and for you both to get to know each other, and how the therapy will work.

In terms of the contract, you will have to sign a counselling contract because this lays out how the therapy sessions work, how your allocation works, what happens if you miss a session, what happens if you need to make a complaint and so on.

This might sound scary but this is a simple document that is designed to protect you as the client and the mental health service.

My counsellor explained the contract in a very easy-to-understand way and it was really nice.

She did something very clever too.

This might sound simple but in my future clinical work, I am definitely doing this with my own clients. She left the contract on the table next to the chair I was sitting on, so I could simply reach over to the contract, get it and read it. The counsellor did not need to move from her chair and she did not need to get close to me in any fashion.

As a survivor, I flat out love that little technique. It made me feel really safe, protected and I was much happier to engage with her. It showed me that she did respect me, she wasn't going to presume anything about my boundaries and she was going to give me the space I needed to heal and process what He had done to me.

I respect that a lot.

Especially, in my traumatised state, I would have had a panic attack, my nervous system would have activated and I would be way too focused on survival instead of the therapy if she had come anywhere near me. That didn't happen so I was happier and calmer.

After explaining the contract, she moved on to the confidentiality section of the first session, which is always good. It basically reaffirms that everything you say within session is completely confidential and will not leave the therapy room unless in a few situations. She will need to tell a safeguarding professional if I am experiencing ongoing sexual violence. As well as in mental health practice, there is something called "Supervision". In supervision, a mental health professional might talk about their caseload with a supervisor to get ideas about how to help the client or if a case is negatively impacting their mental health then they can talk about it in supervision.

In essence, supervision is all about the mental health professional making sure they are okay in the long term so they can keep helping clients.

Information On The Sexual Violence Itself

You don't cover the rape or sexual violence itself in your therapy, at least not directly.

I know for the vast majority of sexual assault survivors, they are very concerned, nervous and anxious about specialist counselling or therapy because they're concerned that they will have to relive the memories of their sexual trauma. Thankfully, in rape counselling, you never have to tell the counsellor exactly what happened to you in any detail.

Since the main focus of rape counselling is

that you focus on stabilising yourself, your nervous system and process the trauma in indirect ways that means you never have to reveal exactly what happened to you.

Personally, I was very surprised about this aspect of the counselling, because I was "happy" to talk about what happened to me. Especially because I thought that was critical to the therapy, but as the sessions have gone on I realised how that wasn't correct. I have done so much healing and therapy working without having to explain my rape in any detail.

The closest I've come to explaining to my counsellor what exactly happened to me was when I was telling her about the situations that led to me meeting my attacker. Then again, she never asked for that information and I only told her because it was useful for context in something I wanted help with.

In addition, at the time of writing, which is a little while after this first session, I helped a good friend of mine access the same rape crisis centre as me. Their main concern was having to tell the counsellor, effectively a stranger, everything that happened to them.

Therefore, when I told my friend that they wouldn't need to reveal any detail of what happened to them. They were a lot more relaxed and happy to progress with the self-referral.

I want *you* to know that you never have to tell your counsellor anything you don't want to. You are in full control of the counselling.

Other Things Of Note

To start wrapping up this chapter, I wanted to mention some of the other things we spoke about in case they're useful to you for context.

My favourite thing that we spoke about was "call it what *you* want. Only you can decide". If you've read my other sexual violence focused books then you'll probably be aware that I've experienced a lot of invalidation surrounding my rape. A lot of people refused to allow me to call it rape and they only wanted me to go by legal definitions because legal definitions made it less severe and less scary for *them*.

Because I was *only* sexually assaulted, I wasn't raped.

In reality, I call it rape because if the guy's dick worked it would have been considering what he tried to do.

Anyway, experiencing constant invalidation and having people deny that I was raped really took a toll on my mental health. It made me feel very isolated, slightly insane and I was gaslighted because I was going through all these PTSD, depression and anxiety symptoms but people were saying the root cause never happened.

That really hurt me.

Therefore, I brought this up in the counselling session and she mentioned that it doesn't matter what other people call it, because it happened to me, it's impacting me and I am the one that is hurting. Only I get to decide what I call it and that thankfully reinforced the conclusion I had already drawn on my own, because as I've researched sexual violence survivors more and more. I've realised how interchangeably the definitions are and can be used depending on how comfortable a survivor is with a particular word.

Moreover, there was a lot of talk about my trauma responses (both sexual and childhood trauma) and she mentioned the 5-Steps to mindfulness. Which is a very good technique focusing on setting you to name 5 things you see, 4 things you can touch, 3 things you can hear, 2 or 1 things you can smell and taste. That helps you to ground yourself in the present moment instead of any trauma memories or flashbacks or trauma responses you're experiencing.

I really do recommend that technique.

Finally, something very small that I appreciated was she reinforced something I was doubting. Ever since I was raped and since my own mental health died as my psychological distress grew to such intensity I was experiencing hourly trauma reactions. Even going outside was problematic. I doubted that I could ever be a clinical psychologist in the future because whenever I heard someone's mental health experience it would cause me extreme levels of distress and it would trigger a very wide range of responses in me.

As a result, I had considered going into academic research because I enjoy it, I'm good at it and I know how to run studies very well. By the end of April 2025, I'm hoping to have run 5 studies in total independent of my Masters, because me and my supervisor at the university get on great so she lets me research a bunch of topics related to transgender mental health.

Nonetheless, at the time, I was scared that this wasn't a valid career path because I didn't know if it was important and I was scared or if this was just a trauma reaction. Thankfully, she reminded me how important research is in psychotherapy and counselling work. Our treatments and interventions have to be evidence-based because it is the evidence-based approaches that save lives.

She made me feel a lot better about that decision.

Ultimately, the first session was brilliant because she made me feel listened to, respected and I could see she was someone I could work with. Sure, I knew it wouldn't be easy in the future and I would struggle because of my trauma but I was interested and driven to heal.

And that was only possible because of a great first session.

WHAT ARE SOME SELF-SOOTHING STRATEGIES?

In the last therapy reflection, I mentioned how my counsellor wanted me to start focusing on self-soothing techniques so **I** could do something to help myself relax when I get distressed. Now the issue I had with this therapy conversation was that I had no idea what self-soothing actually involved and I had no clue how to self-soothe.

I have never ever been good at it before so I needed to learn. Hence, the research and chapter that you're about to read, and these techniques and a few more that my counsellor gave me have been rather life changing.

As a result, the ability to self-soothe is beyond critical to mental health because it allows us to calm ourselves down, we can relax and return to our window of tolerance. Yet some people aren't able to self-soothe so to relax, calm down and maintain their mental health they need others to soothe them. This is a strategy that works for a time but it is far from perfect and it doesn't solve anything.

I struggle a lot with my inability to self-soothe because this was the focus of the topic this week in my specialist counselling session. Therefore, in this chapter, you'll learn what is self-soothing, how can you self-soothe and why it's so important to your mental health.

What Is Self-Soothing?

A person's ability to self-soothe is their efforts to calm themselves down when they're in an emotional state as proposed by Wright (2009). As well as this is beyond critical for our psychological well-being because it helps people to stay calm and emotionally regulated.

I know this is a massive issue for me because my ability to self-soothe has always been bad, but after my rape, over time it got worse and worse. Currently, at the time of writing, I essentially cannot self-soothe at all, which is a massive problem. This is why I'm focusing on this in therapy.

Moreover, a lot of people learn how to self-soothe when we're babies because when our caregivers soothe us, we internalise this soothing and learn how to do it ourselves (Wright, 2009). Yet there are a wide range of reasons why people (like me) are unable to learn these self-soothing skills and use them as adults.

Thankfully, it is perfectly possible to learn how to self-soothe as an adult and that's the focus of this chapter. Granted, self-soothing requires self-insight, we need to develop our skills and we need to be able to effectively use these skills in an effort to calm ourselves down.

This is an important bit I believe because we can read and learn everything we want to about self-soothing. Yet unless we practice and get better *over time* then we will never actually improve our self-soothing skills.

What Are Some Self-Soothing Strategies?

Take Some Deep Breaths

I wanted to start us off with an extremely simple one because I know from personal experience, it is this extremely simple and extremely useful technique that we tend to forget the most. As well as I want to take advantage of the primacy and recency effect. Therefore, whenever we want to self-soothe we need to deactivate our sympathetic nervous system. This means we need to activate our parasympathetic nervous system because this nervous system helps to stop the fight-or-flight response and helps us to calm down.

Thankfully, the parasympathetic nervous system can be very easily activated by taking a few long, deep breaths, including box breathing. Box breathing involves you breathing in for a count of 4 then you hold for a count of 4 and breathe out for a count of 4. Finally, you hold for a count of 4.

You do this a few times until you start to feel calmer.

Again, you need to practice this, so let's try it right now together.

- Breathe in for a count of 4.
- Hold your breath for a count of 4
- Breathe out
- Hold

You would do this a few times but I hope you already start to feel calmer. I know I do.

You Need To Listen To Relaxing Music

Something I've only just realised is that when my mental health is bad and I cannot focus on doing something on my laptop, I play relaxing music as a matter of habit. I never do it when my mental health is good, but I still do it to self-soothe. I never realised that until now. In fact, on YouTube, I'm currently listening to *"Cozy Autumn Vibes, Beautiful Relaxing Music, Peaceful Soothing Instrumental Music, By Tim Janis"*.

It's very good by the way.

Anyway, listening to relaxing music is a good idea for self-soothing because this type of music helps to reduce the stress hormone called Cortisol (Khalfa et al., 2003). As a result, if you're feeling distressed and you're spiralling, try listening to relaxing music because this calming music might help you change your mood, help you to breathe deeper and decrease the negative emotions that you're experiencing.

If you have a Go-To music service that you love (my friends still don't understand why I prefer YouTube for my music over Spotify), then maybe create a playlist of relaxing music so you can listen to it when you're distressed.

Then remember to actually play it and listen to it.

<u>You Should Do Pleasant Activities To Self-Soothe</u>

Personally, I know how difficult, impossible and awful it can be when you're depressed, spiralling or in a mental health crisis, because we all know we need to do pleasant activities to maintain our mental health. Yet when we're spiralling and urgently need to self-soothe, it can be so impossible to do these things that we enjoy.

However, Dialectical Behavioural Therapy suggests that we can self-soothe by doing activities that bring us joy and make us happy (Linehan, 1993). Especially as us doing a pleasurable activity when we're distressed can make us feel better.

As a result, when you're distressed, try to do activities you enjoy. Be it reading, gardening, exercise, whatever. Just try to do something that makes you happy.

When I'm distressed, I try to watch something I'll enjoy, listen to podcasts, cook, read or hang out with friends. Since these are the activities that make me happy and they help to make me feel better. Of course that doesn't mean they're easy to do in the slightest when I'm distressed but over time as you practise to self-soothe more and more then these strategies become a lot easier.

<u>Conclusion</u>

In my opinion, none of these strategies are useful alone and in isolation. In reality, whilst all these are highly effective self-soothing strategies, they feed into each other. For example, when you're distressed you cannot simply start doing pleasurable activities because in my experience, you cannot focus and you cannot enjoy them. Therefore, you can start to self-soothe by doing box-breathing to activate our parasympathetic nervous system so you can calm down or listen to relaxing music. Then you can start to do pleasurable activities to help you self-soothe for longer.

So much of psychology and mental health advice can never be done effectively in isolation.

Therefore, to end this chapter, I want to finish by saying that having an inability to self-soothe can be very damaging to your mental health, and it is so annoying. Yet it is more than possible over time to practise and improve your self-soothing skills. I never thought I would be able to self-soothe but last night I got triggered by a stupid sex ad on YouTube and I got distressed yet I practised box-breathing and managed to self-soothe for the first time in my life.

And I am very proud of myself for managing that.

Now I just need to keep practising, keep trying and keep strengthening my ability to self-soothe. It is possible regardless of how impossible and scary it seems. Just keep trying and using the strategies included in this chapter and one day you will get there.

And it will be a wonderful feeling when you do.

WHAT IS PERSON-CENTRED THERAPY?

In the last chapter, I mentioned that my counsellor was a humanistic counsellor and in my experience, a lot of humanistic counsellors draw on concepts from person-centred therapy. Therefore, in this chapter, adapted from a psychology article from The Psychology World Podcast, you'll learn what is person-centred therapy, some of my own experiences and what you might experience as you engage with a humanistic counsellor or therapist.
Enjoy.

***

Interestingly enough in August 2023, I started four weeks of psychotherapy to help me deal with trauma and abuse from my past and I have only recently learnt that the counsellor (or as I call her 'therapist') uses a person-centred approach to therapy. I have only just heard about this approach to mental health to be honest, so I want to explore it further. Since I found it rather useful. Therefore, in this clinical psychology podcast episode, we'll explore what is person-centred therapy, how does it work, what to expect and so much more.

What Is Person-Centred Psychotherapy?

Person-centred therapy is a client-based psychotherapy that uses a non-authoritative approach to mental health difficulties that allows clients to take the lead in therapy sessions so they can discover their own solutions to their difficulties.

This particular approach to mental health was started by Carl Rodgers because he believed that every person is unique (which we are) and everyone's view of their world should be trusted. In other words, he believed we should never ever doubt our clients and how they describe the world, because to them that actually is how the world works.

Personally, I do understand this because everyone interprets different situations and events differently depending on their past experiences. This is basically what the cognitive approach is saying just with different words. Due to the cognitive approach believes it isn't the events themselves that cause mental health difficulties it is our beliefs and interpretations of them that lead to difficulties.

Furthermore, Carl Rodgers firmly believed in self-actualisation. This is the idea that all of us have the solutions, knowledge and power to make the changes we need in our lives. As well as this therapy is non-directive so the therapist doesn't take the lead and instead follows the client and doesn't engage in any direct discussions.

However, something I am seriously starting to notice is that all these different approaches to mental health are basically just rehashing what another has already said. For example, every single psychotherapy I can think of is about self-actualisation and making sure the client realises *they* can make the changes needed in their lives using the tools and guidance the therapist gives them. Yet only they can make the changes for themselves.

This actually isn't unique to any approach.

Moreover, I will admit that the non-directive part of person-centred therapy does require a bit of getting used to. Since I love cognitive-behavioural therapy, which is very structured, I had to let go of the idea that she was going to lead, and I had to lead instead. Thankfully I have so much mental health difficulties tied up in different parts of abuse and trauma that I have more than enough things to talk about, but it still did require a bit of relearning.

Anyway, during person-centred therapy, a therapist isn't the lead as we know. Instead the therapist is known as a "compassionate facilitator" because they listen to the client without judgement, they acknowledge the client's experiences without changing or moving the conversation and they are there to support the client without interrupting them. Or impacting on their own process of self-discovery.

In my experience that acknowledgement and "validation" in a fashion is extremely important and it does feel great to have someone else call your abuse and trauma, well, abuse and trauma. And I will happily admit that the process of self-discovery it is scary how much you can actually discover about yourself when we free yourself up. Like I literally cannot share everything I've discovered about myself on the podcast because that's like another twenty episodes in itself, but it's a lot of fun. And honestly, as much as really don't want to discover anything more about myself, I know I will and that's okay.

Overall, the reason why the therapist doesn't interrupt this process of self-discovery and lead is because it is down to the client to uncover what hurts them and what they need to do to repair it. That is a very powerful realisation when it hits you.

How Does Person-Centred Therapy Work?

The entire point of person-centred therapy is to step away from the more traditional psychotherapeutic models where the therapist is the leader and expert and instead the client is the expert in themselves. Again that is something I have mentioned a thousand times before on the podcast and in books.

Therefore, person-centred therapy has three central tenets that allow the therapy to be successful. Firstly, the therapist has an unconditional positive regard so they are empathetic and non-judgemental. Due to the therapist accepts what the client is saying as true and they want to convey to the client that they are understood, confident, trusted and they are valued. As well as the client is free to make their own better choices and decisions in their life.

This tenet I think is very powerful and helpful because I have tried to talk about my past before and there are only ever three outcomes really. None of which I blame on people. Firstly, they call me a liar because they don't want to hear it because what I have to say is too painful. Secondly, they are sorry for what's happening but they can ultimately never ever understand it at a deep level. Thirdly, they understand it but the problem with that is it is common trauma and abuse so they aren't comfortable listening to it and because of emotional dependency and other difficulties, I burn them out too much.

That's why having a therapist that can just listen to me talk is extremely helpful.

Secondly, there is congruence or

genuineness so the therapists have no air of authority to them. Instead they present themselves as an accessible and their true self that clients can see is honest and transparent. And this is definitely true, I might be autistic so reading and understanding people is always going to be hard but I know my therapist is very honest and transparent.

Finally, there is empathetic understanding where the therapist wholeheartedly accepts and understands the client's views as well as feelings in a way that can be helpful in reshaping the client's sense of their experiences.

Normally, I think this final part is done by "accident" in a fashion because just by talking and listening and offering up good psychological insights. My therapist has helped me to realise a lot about myself and how I view my Self and my past and my relationships.

On the whole, in this therapy, whenever the therapy is working well the clients feel they are better understood in these sessions and this leads them to feel better understood in other areas of their lives as well. This does have research support, especially whenever a client identifies the unconditional positive regard in their therapist there is an increased chance in positive outcomes. Since the therapeutic relationship between the therapist and the client is a type of therapy in itself.

When Is Person-Centred Therapy Used?

A person-centred therapeutic approach might be used with groups and individuals, be it adults or adolescents in a short- or long-term fashion. The people that tend to take this approach and benefit from it are people that want more self-confidence, a stronger sense of identity and authenticity, increased trust in their own relationships and more success in establishing (and maintaining I will add) their interpersonal relationships.

In addition, like other approaches to mental health, the person-centred approach doesn't have to be used only because it can be combined with other therapies to treat depression, grief and anxiety. Although, it can also be treated to treat trauma, family stressors, abuse and so much more.

And because this is a client-led psychotherapy, it is the more motivated and determined clients that tend to do better and be more successful at the therapy.

Personally, even though I didn't choose person-centred therapy, I am more than glad I ended up with it. Since I've only had two sessions so far and I have found it so useful in understanding my own relationships, my identity, self-confidence and it has basically taught me to let go of what other people want from me and their expectations. I talk about this a little more next week in the Emotional Dependency and Locus of Evaluation podcast episode but person-centred therapy has been immensely useful to me.

What To Expect In Person-Centred Therapy?

Even though I've mentioned my own experience through the podcast episode, the only other thing I want to say is that the therapist might repeat your words. This isn't them trying to be annoying or anything, it is simply them trying to understand what happened, what you mean and how you feel. It is them trying to draw out a little more information from you too.

Of course, they might have misunderstood you and I think that's happened once or twice with myself. One time was when, because I laugh as a coping mechanism when I have seriously screwed up, she didn't understand why I was laughing about something extremely serious (well at least it was to me). This allowed me to rephrase my response in a way both of us could understand.

Moreover, there might be moments of silence in the therapy and this can be good because it allows us to process our thoughts and realisations. Since person-centred therapy is all about self-acceptance and self-discovery. Or if you're like me and you have so many things to unpack, you basically don't stop talking for the entire session.

Then you end up at the end of the therapy feeling a little overwhelmed because of everything you've learnt, discussed and it can take a little while for you to realise what the takeaways are for you.

<u>Conclusion</u>

Overall, person-centred therapy is all about allowing a client to talk, explore their difficulties and find the solutions for themselves. This is extremely helpful in my experience but then again I've learnt recently I have very high emotional intelligence, which is funny because I used to be extremely bad at it.

A Person-centred Therapist should always have the ability to be calm in sessions and they need to let a client verbalise their frustrations and disappointments too. Since this can all help a client to gain insights into what's hurting them and most importantly how they can move forwards.

Personally, I am willing to say that person-centred therapy has already changed my life for the better and I still have two more sessions, so I am actually really excited to see what will happen, what will I learn and most importantly how else can *I* change my life for the better.

Therapy can be seriously fun, interesting and life changing if you want it to be.

WINDOW OF TOLERANCE, SOCIAL SCRIPTS AND CHILD TRAUMA HEALING: LESSONS LEARNT FROM A SECOND SESSION

There were a lot of technology issues between the first and second session of my specialist counselling. My counsellor was meant to send me a bunch of things but when I didn't get them, I was feeling let down and I was nervous about how good my counsellor actually was. Yet thankfully, she had sent them, there was just an issue with the email so I never got them.

Therefore, in the next chapter of the book, I will explain Window Of Tolerance a lot more and in a lot more detail, but we focused on this topic by me watching a video that she had sent me. I didn't mind spending the first 6 minutes (I watch videos on 2-times speed) of the session watching the video because I wanted to try and I knew this was a useful concept.

In essence, Window Of Tolerance is about the area of stress we can handle and function in without trauma reactions kicking in and making us anxious and fear or depressed and us freezing.

That is a very cruel explanation of the topic but in the next chapter, you get to explore this topic in a lot more depth.

In addition, we spent a lot of time on Window of Tolerance, because it's a useful psychoeducation tool. It teaches you about the body's reactions, the nervous system and *why* we have trauma responses after sexual trauma. Once this was explained to me, I was much "happier" because I know my body's reactions weren't my fault. It was simply my body reacting in normal ways for an extremely abnormal situation.

After you read the next chapter, you'll find it really useful too.

Moreover, in the second session, I mentioned how when I start shaking, getting anxious and terrified because of a trigger. I tried to stop the shaking in its tracks, which my counsellor said might not be a useful thing to do. Due to the body shakes because it's released adrenaline into the bloodstream and that extra energy that the hormone gives you needs to go somewhere. Hence, the shaking so when I try to stop this I'm storing up that energy.

Instead it's a good idea to simply allow my body to shake, release that energy and adrenaline and everything will be fine.

At the time, I was rather surprised by her saying that it was useful to know, and I did tend to find that after I started doing this technique (if you can call it that) that my shaking was shorter and the aftermath wasn't so intense. It was useful.

Furthermore, during the first half of my counselling sessions I was severely anxious, depressed and I was not having a good time at all. Every single night without fail I would get depressed, my anxiety would skyrocket and I would be constantly plagued with intrusive thoughts, physical sensations and nightmares that I would be getting raped over and over again.

It was awful.

That was my life every single night for 7 months. At the time of my second session, it had been 5 months since my rape so I was going to suffer and my mental health was going to get a lot worse in the next two months. Honestly, I didn't even think that was possible at the time.

As a result, I mentioned this to my counsellor and she mentioned it might be a good idea if I have a "Good Things" box. This is a box, be it physical or digital like a folder on a phone, that is filled with things that make you smile and help you when you're having a bad day. For example, you might want to fill it with pictures of loved ones, friends and good memories. Equally, you could fill it with loving and positive messages, basically anything that makes you happy.

It is all about having and being able to access good things that make you feel better when you're having a bad day.

Therefore, I included things like pictures of my best friend, good days out, messages from friends and loved ones over the years and positive messages from my readers that make me happy.

I highly recommend that you do this too because as a survivor, you will have bad days (probably a lot of them) and you will need the positivity. I know that so please create a box or something you can access when you need it most.

Before I talk about the third counselling session, we'll learn about *How To Survive A Major Depressive Episode* to give you some extra techniques too in case you experience an episode. Something I did for about two- to three months because of my rape.

Childhood Trauma and Social Scripts

Something you need to know about me is that I suffered a decade of unintentional abuse and intense homophobia. My family flat out hated gay people and thought gay people were the scum of the earth. One side of my family was deeply religious and the other side just didn't care enough about gay people to defend them or say anything nice about them.

It wasn't exactly abnormal for me to hear "we need to beat the gay out of them" at least once a week and then there were all the other homophobic comments in between. As well as there are the very public outrage that my parents had whenever they used to see a gay couple, let alone a transgender couple, in public.

It was rough and that utter fear and terror that I felt every single day of my life for a decade took a massive toll on my mental health. This went on for about a decade before I had a massive breakdown, got immensely suicidal and my life fell apart. My family had to get better at supporting me and being less homophobic.

It took my rape to stop it completely.

I mention this about my life and childhood that I've written a lot about in other places, because this directly impacted my trauma recovery for my rape. All the trauma, pain and lessons I had learnt during my childhood just to survive was impeding my trauma healing even more.

Especially, as I believed that if my family found out I was gay then I would be beaten, kicked out of my house or worse.

This was made even worse by my family constantly invalidating my trauma, and telling me that my rape wasn't impacting me as much as it was and I simply needed to move on.

Who the hell can just "move on" after being raped?

In addition, the typical advice recommended for the families and friends of rape survivors is to research sexual violence, sexual trauma and investigate how to help the survivor as much as possible whilst looking after yourself too. My family are not the type of people to actually do that no matter how much I'm struggling, jumping at any sound and my trauma responses getting worse and worse.

They wouldn't help me.

This continued to have a greater and greater impact on my mental health, so I mentioned it in counselling.

We had a long conversation about my family, my childhood trauma and what I needed to do now about it. The conclusion was that because I was scared of standing up to them, because if I did that in my childhood then I would be shouted at, berated and accused of a bunch of stuff. The issue was that I didn't have boundaries with them, because I would set them, they would step over them and I would get too scared of them to stand up to my family.

That is a major difficulty after sexual violence that lots of survivors have, it is even worse if you never developed setting boundaries anyway.

Also, it's worth noting that my family blames me for everything that happens in regards to my mental health. It was my fault I was raped, my rape was a "lesson learnt" about not being gay, me being suicidal and scared of my family because they were actively telling me they wanted to beat up gay people, that was all my fault.

They will never take responsibility for

their actions.

As a result, towards the end of the session, we spoke about setting boundaries with them, the importance of reinforcing boundaries they crossed and developing social scripts so I knew what to say when things didn't go to plan.

This is what I explore in two later chapters about family boundaries and healing from childhood trauma.

As a result, whilst over the next week, this caused me a lot of concern and fear because for the first time ever I was going to tell my family some boundaries so I could heal, I learnt a lot.

I did a lot of online research which is where the next few family-based chapters come from, as well as I found the following online:

- What boundaries do I want to set?
- What could their responses be?
- Write down everything parents have done that's crossed a boundary
- How will I keep myself safe?
- Train yourself to counter these responses

Personally, I highly recommend that you think about these questions and you write down your answers. This will allow you to always check-in with yourself about what your boundaries are, and they will help remind you why boundaries are important, and why and how your family crosses them.

This is a great, but tough, exercise to do. I really benefited from it though so I hope it can help you as well.

To wrap up this therapy session that seriously benefited my mental health in the long-term, I wanted to share with you a text message that I sent a family member after they accidentally crossed a boundary two days before. This was the first time I stuck up for myself and it is this text that changed our relationship for the better as it led to a longer conversation.

"Hi, how's work? Is *Co-Worker* still there?

I've had some good times this week. I finished making my Outreach lecture, seminar and library research task on How To reduce Reoffending? As part of a Degree for A Day programme. A Whitstable school has already booked the event for Jan/ Feb. I'm excited.

And I hung out with *New Friend* and *Best Friend* for over 3 hours on Tuesday. Which was really fun and good considering.

Also, it was lovely you calling me Friday to check if I was the stabbing victim *(Context, there are a stabbing in my local area)*. Yet please remember what I said to you about checking up on me. Please do check up on me because I love you and I enjoy talking to you, but if you're going to check on me please actually hear how I am. Because you don't know about my eating disorder and that's the main way I'm struggling this week.

And me and *Best Friend* are going into Canterbury today to enjoy some French cafe food. It'll be really good."

It might not be the most naturally worded text I've ever sent but it was important, because it led to a texting conversation about how I was really struggling, what I needed from my family and so on.

It is immensely scary setting boundaries but it is so, so worth it in the long-term as you will see in the following chapters.

WHAT IS WINDOW OF TOLERANCE?

Normally as an aspiring clinical psychologist, I don't really focus too much on how our biological processes and the nervous system impacts our mental health. I should focus on this area a lot more than I do because our physical reactions to trauma, anxiety and depression are very important. Instead I tend to focus on the psychological processes that interact with our physical processes to produce behaviours. Yet as I deal with my sexual trauma more and more, I've realised I can no longer ignore the impact our nervous system and the role it plays in our mental health.

Therefore, in this chapter, we'll be focusing on window of tolerance, hyperarousal and hypoarousal during psychological distress. And how importantly we can get back within our window of tolerance to improve our mental health. If you enjoy learning about clinical psychology, biological psychology and the nervous system then you'll love this chapter.

What Is The Window of Tolerance?

This is a topic that has been critical in my rape counselling and once I understood this psychological concept, things started to get a little easier. You or your clients understanding the window of tolerance isn't a magic bullet that will suddenly make everything better but it can be immensely useful in healing from trauma, including sexual violence.

Therefore, Window of Tolerance was a term coined by Daniel J. Siegel who was a clinical professor at the UCLA School of Medicine. He created Window of Tolerance to describe the optimal emotional "zone" that people can best exist in so they can thrive and function in their everyday lives. When someone is within their Window of Tolerance then they have a sense of groundedness, openness, curiosity, presence, flexibility, an ability to emotionally self-regulate and a capacity to tolerate any stressors that pop up in their everyday life.

However, either side of the Window of Tolerance are two different states where we do not function and thrive in our daily lives. These states are called the hypoarousal and hyperarousal states.

When someone is in hyperarousal then they are in an emotional state that we can characterise as panic, anger, high energy, anxiety, irritability, overwhelm, chaos, hypervigilance, startle responses and fight-or-flight instincts. For example, I know I'm in a hyperarousal state running my panic attacks, anxiety and my thoughts running a million miles an hour about how unsafe I am and how I need to escape or I am going to die or get raped again.

On the other end of the spectrum is the hypoarousal state where someone effectively shuts down and experiences numbness, withdrawal, depressiveness, flat affect, disconnection, shame amongst others. For instance, when I'm in a hypoarousal state (like an hour before I started writing this post), I was severely depressed, shut down and I didn't want to move. I effectively wanted to play dead so I couldn't be hurt again like he did to me that night.

Why Is The Window of Tolerance Important?

If we are outside of our Window of Tolerance then we cannot function and thrive in our everyday lives. For example, when my mental health died in August and September (and probably October) 2024 because of my rape, most of the time I was too hypervigilance, anxious and terrified to function on most days. I was always in a state of hyperarousal, or I was too depressed and shut down to function (hypoarousal).

Therefore, when we're in our Window of Tolerance, we can access all the prefrontal cortex as well as executive functioning skills we need to be able to thrive. Like, our ability to organise, plan and prioritise complex tasks that we need to complete. Also, being within our Window of Tolerance means we can emotionally self-regulate, start projects and actions and focus on them and practice good time management.

These executive functions are critical to our functioning because they allow us to work, problem-solve whatever issues and challenges we face and they allow us to be present and work in our relationships.

This is a major problem I had during my mental health crisis. I was too anxious, terrified or depressed to do much work, problem-solve and I wasn't able to have or maintain many social relationships. I wasn't able to do much Outreach work at my university because a lot of it was brand-new students and staff that I had never worked with before, and the specific type of Outreach activities, because it was the school holidays, were so different to what I was used to. I couldn't deal with it.

Then it was even worse for my own business. I couldn't write as much, I couldn't do a fraction of the business tasks that I needed to do and I can see the impact it has on my bottom line and the podcast audience.

This is why being within our Window of Tolerance is so important.

Moreover, we lose access to these skills when we're outside of our Window of Tolerance because we lose access to the prefrontal cortex and our executive skills. Since instead of relying on these brain areas, we default to panic, action or a freeze response. Sometimes this can even manifest as self-sabotaging behaviours so we might gravitate towards choices and patterns that undermine or erode our relationship with ourselves, others and the world.

Ultimately, it's important that we try to stay within our Window of Tolerance so we can support ourselves, function and live in a healthy way. Yet there will always be times in our lives when we fall outside our Window of Tolerance and we end up in some non-deal emotionally regulated way.

Thankfully, this is just a part of human behaviour and it's natural and normal.

Therefore, the ultimate goal of this chapter isn't to make sure we never ever fall outside of our Window of Tolerance. That is never going to happen, but instead I want to show you why it's important to expand our Window of Tolerance. This allows a person to effectively bounce back quicker and be more resilient over time, so we can better deal with being outside our Window of Tolerance.

In my opinion, this is a critical area of mental health and trauma work because as my Window of Tolerance has expanded I have been able to deal with more and more. For example, I used to have thousands of triggers (probably not a joke) but everything has been toned down recently in terms of my PTSD. Like a few months ago, if I even saw a reference of sex in a film or book, my mental health completely died and I would have major intrusive thoughts and flashbacks. Now I can tolerate sex references and even the odd light sex scene in a film or book and I only experience mild intrusive thoughts and flashbacks.

It's still a little distressing but it is nowhere near as bad as in the past few months.

How Do You Increase Your Window of Tolerance?

Whilst there are several effective therapeutic techniques and activities that can over time increase your Window of Tolerance, everyone's Window of Tolerance is rather different because of a range of biopsychosocial factors. For example, whether or not you have childhood trauma and social support can impact the size of your Window of Tolerance as well as your physiology, personal history and your temperament.

All these factors and more interact with each other to make your Window of Tolerance, and no two Windows of Tolerance will ever be the same.

As a result, it's important to mention that people, like me, who come from trauma backgrounds will have a smaller Window of Tolerance than people who have not experienced trauma. This shrinking of the Window of Tolerance isn't unique to any type of trauma, like physical, childhood or sexual trauma, your Window of Tolerance doesn't discriminate. Trauma is trauma and it is the unfortunate gift that keeps on giving.

The reason why trauma shrinks your Window of Tolerance is because trauma gives you triggers that are more likely to rapidly and more frequently push you outside your Window of Tolerance and into hypoarousal or hyperarousal.

Consequently, it's important that as part of trauma work (even though anyone can benefit from this knowledge) is that we work to expand a client's Window of Tolerance. This allows the client to practice resilience and bring themselves back into their Window of Tolerance when you're in a hypoarousal or hyperarousal state. The only reason difference in this regard between people with and without trauma is that a person with relational trauma might need to work worker, longer and dedicate more time and effort into expanding their Window of Tolerance.

Personally, I can relate to this because it is normal for a person's Window of Tolerance to expand as they get older, experience more things and stressors, and they learn more techniques without realising it about to bring themselves back into their Window of Tolerance. However, ever since I was raped up until 7 months later when I learnt how to feel safe in my own body. I just couldn't bring myself back into my Window of Tolerance and it required a lot of therapeutic work, a lot of effort and a lot longer than I wanted to to be able to bring myself reliably back into my Window of Tolerance.

There are still times I cannot achieve this but 90% of the time I thankfully can.

In addition, there are two main ways how someone can recognise that their Windows of Tolerance are unique and how to expand it. Ultimately, we need to understand the foundational biopsychosocial elements that contribute to a healthy nervous system and that's why I flat out love *Healing Sexual Trauma Workbook* by Erika Shershun because it handles this topic very well. Also, we can give ourselves this knowledge by providing our minds with supportive experiences. This can include providing ourselves with good amounts of stimulation, focus and engagement whilst we balance this with good amounts of play, rest and spaciousness. This was a mistake I made this week at the time of writing because I overbooked myself with Outreach work at my university so I had plenty of stimulation, focus and I was really engaged with helping students change their lives, but I didn't give myself enough rest time.

Hence, I found myself very outside my Window of Tolerance on two occasions this week.

Moreover, we need to provide our bodies with supportive self-care. For example, we need to get enough sleep, exercise, eat nutritious foods, attend to our medical needs and avoid substances that damage our health. Since if our bodies aren't looked after then our nervous system won't be healthy and it will be easier to go outside our Window of Tolerance. As well as we need to provide ourselves with supportive experiences like being in a connected relationship and being connected to something bigger than ourselves.

I know this sounds like religion and I suppose some people find this helpful, but you can be connected to other things greater than yourself. For example, I connect to my Outreach work at my university because I'm helping to inspire and show young people that it doesn't matter what background or area they come from, if they want to they can go to university and thrive. As well as I connect to my books and my podcast because I am providing people with a psychology education, entertainment and hopefully I'll inspire some people to enjoy mental health and clinical psychology as much as I do.

You can connect to anything that you are passionate about.

Finally for this first part, you can tend to your physical environment to set yourself up for success. You can do this by working and living in places and ways that reduce your stressors instead of increasing them. As well as you can design an external environment that nourishes you instead of depletes you. I did this when I moved into my shared house with my best friend back in June because as one of our housemates wasn't moving in for another 3 months, I made their room my office (with their permission) and that was great for me. It gave me a stress-free, non-triggering environment for me to do what I loved.

Secondly, we need to work with ourselves to cultivate and use a wide range of tools to bring ourselves back inside our Window of Tolerance when we inevitably find ourselves outside. You can do this by developing tools, habits, practices and internalised and externalised resources that help you to self-soothe, self-regulate and ground yourself. I'm smiling as I write as I write this because these are aspects of Window of Tolerance that I've been reading about lately in Erika Shershun's book, and it's very helpful to learn about.

Maybe I'll dive into these aspects of Window of Tolerance in a future chapter.

Conclusion

I cannot stress enough the importance of Window of Tolerance in trauma work, because it actually did change my life. There are a lot of concepts in clinical psychology that are useful to some clients but not all, and there are certain concepts that are useful to the vast, vast majority of clients. Window of Tolerance is certainly one of the latter, because it is a very useful tool for psychoeducation and explaining to trauma explains why their body is reacting in the ways that it is.

It was a relief to understand why my body was doing all these extreme trauma responses and it was nice to put a name to the psychological framework. Therefore, it meant now I understood what I was dealing with it, I could research, read and practice how to expand my Window of Tolerance and how to reduce the volatility of my nervous system.

If I didn't know about Window of Tolerance, I certainly wouldn't be as far along in my recovery as I am now.

Ultimately, the Window of Tolerance might "only" be a psychoeducational concept but it is an extremely powerful tool to use in clinical trauma work. Therefore, I unofficially suggest to my fellow aspiring and qualified psychologists that you embody this Window of Tolerance in your own life and especially in your clinical trauma work. Your clients and yourself will openly find it more useful and life-changing than you ever thought possible.

I know I did, and that's one of the entire points of our profession.

Clinical psychology is all about changing one life for the better at a time.

HOW TO HEAL FROM FAMILY TRAUMA BY SETTING BOUNDARIES?

In the last chapter I mentioned how I needed to start learning how to deal with family trauma a lot more and the next two chapters are the result of my research and my efforts to thankfully try and build better relationships with my family.

Since when it comes to healing from family trauma, it's flat out critical to learn how to set effective boundaries. These boundaries allow you to heal, protect yourself and build healthier relationships with family members that might have treated you badly before. Their bad or inappropriate treatment doesn't always have to be intentional or malicious, but it can be. My abuse wasn't intentionally malicious but it had done a lot of psychological damage to me over the past decade. As well as it was massively amplified by my rape, and even if you haven't been through additional trauma as you try and heal from the damaging impact of dysfunctional families, setting boundaries is beyond critical. Therefore, in this clinical psychology podcast episode, you'll learn why setting boundaries is important with family members, how to do it and more. If you enjoy learning about trauma healing, distributional families and now then this is a great episode for you.

How Does Setting Boundaries Help Heal Family Trauma?

The reason why setting boundaries helps clients to heal from family trauma is because by setting boundaries, you're helping yourself and other people to understand what is and what is not okay in your relationship. As well as with you being an adult child, it means you have a lot of freedom to set boundaries and limits with your family that will help you to improve your relationships over time. For example, you could set a limit on how much time and energy you invest with them. Also, you setting boundaries might involve invoking your right to self-care and personal autonomy and this is perfectly okay even if it does mean creating a certain distance from particular family members.

Additionally, by setting boundaries, you aren't saying that you don't love your family. Instead setting boundaries means that you are trying to stay connected as well as have a healthy, mature relationship with your family.

Of course, it is worth noting that unfortunately some people just aren't able to have healthy relationships so you may need to distance yourself from them.

Moreover, it's important to know that your boundaries act as a protective shield around you so you are less likely to be hurt by the dysfunctional, immature relationship that your family trauma has caused. Ultimately, setting boundaries with family members helps to protect yourself against further harm and they allow you to reclaim a sense of agency over your life.

And because this is a topic that I struggle a lot with, I want to stress here that asserting your own needs might be incredibly scary but it is so important. Asserting your needs helps you to break free from the patterns of dysfunction as well as co-dependency that effectively made up your upbringing.

I talk about this struggle more in my Work-In-Progress book that focuses on my rape counselling. When I first had the conversation with my Mum about what I needed, the struggles I was facing and everything I was dealing with. I was shaking, terrified and I felt sick, but it worked out okay and everything has improved in the past week. Of course, there will always be challenges ahead but it is progress and it is the small victories you need to celebrate.

How Else Can Boundaries Help Trauma Healing?

Some other ways how setting boundaries can help clients heal from family trauma includes reduced stress. Setting boundaries helps to reduce stress because let's face it, toxic family interactions are extremely draining so boundaries help you to manage the level of stress that these interactions create and you can limit your exposure to these interactions. Therefore, you can focus on your health and wellbeing instead of focusing on the fallout and draining nature of these toxic interactions.

Secondly, setting boundaries can help your sense of safety because boundaries give you a safe space to heal. Since by limiting contact with toxic family members as well as friends and any other toxic people in your life, you can minimise any further emotional harm. I definitely agree with this point because as bad as my mental health is at the time of writing, setting boundaries and expectations with my family has given me one less concern or stressor in my life. This means I can focus, heal and think about other things instead of negative interactions, and I'm already seeing how my interactions with my family are becoming a lot more positive and better for my mental health.

Thirdly, setting boundaries can help to reduce your triggers because toxic family members tend to engage in behaviours that trigger your negative memories or negative emotions. As a result, boundaries help to minimise your exposure to these triggers so you can process your past trauma in a safe and controlled environment. And this is a great point because there have been times when my family have seriously triggered me because of my sexual trauma with some comments, a non-consensual touch or hug and some invalidation. Yet because I set boundaries, I have to deal with these triggers less and that has had a good impact on my mental health.

In addition, self-care is a great benefit of setting boundaries, because boundaries help you to focus on your own mental health and wellbeing. As well as boundaries allow you to treat yourself with the respect and kindness you deserve and this is a critical part of healing from trauma. Something I am needing to get better at. Also, boundaries can free up your time, energy and even money so you can partake in healing activities.

Building upon the last point, setting boundaries helps you to improve your self-esteem because boundaries help you to communicate and truly *feel* your self-worth. Because I know firsthand how people not respecting your boundaries, your consent and your self-worth makes you feel useless, awful and like dirt. Yet you are worth so much, you are clever, brilliant and a great person who deserves so much more. Therefore, by communicating your healthy boundaries, you are showing that you deserve to be treated respectfully by others and you will never tolerate being mistreated ever again.

This reminds me to mention that you need to reinforce your boundaries too, but that's something we mention again later.

Finally, setting boundaries helps you to break the cycle of dysfunction in your life. Since dysfunctional family dynamics and patterns of behaviour are often passed down the generations so setting boundaries helps to disrupt this cycle. Thus, you can build healthier relationships that focus on respect and genuine connection instead of these maladaptive dysfunctional patterns of behaviour.

As well as it's useful to note that every time you stand up for yourself by focusing on your own health and wellbeing, you are becoming a powerful example for future generations. Due to you are truly showing it is possible to overcome these dysfunctional family patterns of behaviour.

<u>How To Deal With Resistant Family Members?</u>

As much as I wish I could tell you that all your family members will be perfectly happy with you setting boundaries, I cannot. There will be a few or maybe the majority of toxic family members and loved ones that think you are being outrageous, unfair and evil for wanting to set boundaries. For example, my family was annoyed at me and very defensive at first when it came to me setting boundaries because everything was my fault.

Furthermore, the strategies that your toxic family members use on you, like guilt, will make you enforcing your boundaries even more difficult. Since you'll be dealing with your own fears of abandonment, guilt and familial duty and loyalty. As well as you might have to deal with internalised core beliefs about that family harmony is more important than your own wellbeing. It is not, but you may still have to deal with those beliefs.

Again, I was utterly terrified when I started to put boundaries in place with my own family because I was scared of being shouted at, hated and being guilt-tripped into submission.

However, there are strategies to help you overcome and deal with resistant family members.

<u>What Are Some Strategies To Deal With Resistant Family Members?</u>

Firstly, you need to start small. This is something my best friend kept banging on about because they could see how distressed and scared I was about setting boundaries, so they encouraged me to start very small. You should start small because this helps make the task of setting boundaries more manageable and then you can gradually build from there. For instance, the only real boundaries I have currently set with my family is something along the lines of *Don't ask me how I am if you aren't going to listen.* That is a very small and manageable boundary that I can and will build on over time.

Think about a small boundary you could set and go from there. Rome wasn't built in a day so neither will boundary setting.

Secondly, you need to be clear and direct. To do this, you should use "I" statements so no one can accuse you of being influenced by other people and you are definitely saying this is what *you* want during this conversation. This is very important in setting your boundaries. For example, you could say the following to your family, "I don't feel comfortable having this conversation right now. I want to take a break and we can talk about this again in the future,"

Thirdly, you need to focus on yourself. As much as I would love to tell you that you can control how others will react that isn't possible and you can only control your own responses as well as actions. It reminds me of something that happened in my friendship group back in May 2024 when a person with persecutory delusions attacked me very publicly and repeatedly over text. I knew right in this moment she was in the wrong for attacking me and I could have ripped into her just as hard but that wouldn't have helped the situation. If I had attacked her back then everything would have gotten a lot worse and there was a very good risk I would become just as guilty as her. My point is what you do when family members are being resistant and possibly attacking you when you go to set boundaries matters. Don't engage, don't make things worse.

If your family members are being resistant and horrible then please, just walk away. You can always return to conversations later on when they are calmer.

Always focus on meeting your own needs and not the needs of others. Sometimes people will change, sometimes they will not so don't waste your energy getting people to change when they will not.

Fourthly, expect pushback. I hope by this point in the podcast episode that you're starting to realise that you will get pushback because toxic family members will not like you setting boundaries and reclaiming your life. Therefore, expect that they're going to manipulate, guilt-trip and use other strategies to try to get you to back down. Yet you need to stay firm, set and enforce those boundaries and take all the time and space you need so you can heal.

This is about you, not them.

Finally, you need to seek support. Not only from a dear friend or non-toxic family member that knows what you're going through, but healing from trauma is hard. It is very possible to heal from trauma but you never have to do it alone. Therefore, please seek support from a therapist, a dear friend and a support group.

Setting boundaries is just one part of the journey towards healing from trauma, but it is a very rewarding part indeed.

Conclusion

Ultimately, when it comes to setting boundaries, it is extremely important to your trauma healing and your life that you never give up. Sure, there will be struggles, setbacks and there will be family members that never want you to set boundaries, but you need to do it for you. You are so much more important than you realise.

Also, it's important to realise, truly realise that healing isn't linear. There will be setbacks, you will dip and you will rise so high that you think the worst is behind you, and that's okay. That is how healing works. I know that better than most.

As a result, I would suggest that you learn from your setbacks and you celebrate your successes. Every single step you take towards healthier boundaries is a step closer towards you creating a space within yourself and within your social world where you can develop self-compassion, post-traumatic growth and you can heal.

Healing is more than possible as much as it seems impossible most of the time, but if you set boundaries then you might be a lot closer to starting to truly heal than you ever thought possible.

WHAT ARE SOCIAL SCRIPTS TO HELP SET FAMILY BOUNDARIES AFTER TRAUMA?

Building upon the last chapter, in this next chapter, you're going to learn the sort of things to say to family members to help set and reinforce your boundaries.

What Are Social Scripts Important?

Social scripts are lines or sentences you practise so you know what to say to family members or other people you are trying to set boundaries with. As well as social scripts are sentences you remember so you can counter and practise defending your boundaries against family resistance.

For example, a boundary I want to set is something along the lines of *if you're going to ask me how I am, actually let me talk about how I actually am*. Yet my "social environment" would have a lot of different excuses about why they shouldn't or wouldn't do that. Mostly it boils down to my trauma is too painful for them, so me being depressed, having PTSD and being suicidal at times is too much for them.

Therefore, developing useful and effective social scripts would allow me to come up with a good counterargument or statement.

Ultimately, survivors of developmental trauma typically experience some form of unsafe, unsupportive and unhealthy family dynamics. This is why as a survivor of trauma, you need to establish boundaries with your family to protect yourself and chances are, they will improve your family relationships too. Yet this can feel like one of the hardest things you will ever do.

To be honest, the night my counsellor recommended this to me I had such a bad mental health spiral because I was so terrified of this idea, and I've been uncomfortable about this setting boundaries idea for days now. Thankfully, I see my "social environment" tomorrow so I can set one or two small boundaries then, I seriously hope I can.

As a result in the rest of this chapter, we'll going to be looking at some scripts you can use in different situations to help set and reinforce your boundaries.

General Social Scripts

In a moment, we're going to look at some social scripts to protect you and set boundaries during specific topics. Yet I want to start us off with some general social scripts that will help you in everyday conversations if your family members try to disrespect your boundaries.

Some general social scripts are:

- *I don't have to explain myself to you.*
- *I prefer not to say.*
- *No, that's why I'm not going to share.*
- *No.*
- *Silence (just don't say anything)*
- *I can't do this, I'm sorry.*

Scripts For Emotionally Charged Conversations

There are certain conversations that will be very emotionally charged, causing yourself and/ or your family members to be very emotional and reactive. These conversations can include death, politics and trauma. For example, my "social environment" firmly denies they have ever done anything wrong whatsoever, so trauma is a very, very emotionally charged topic. Mainly, it involves a lot of gaslighting.

Although, when it comes to these emotionally charged conversations YOU get to decide how you contribute and interact with these topics. You don't actually have to and then you need to communicate your choices to your family members.

Some possible scripts include:

- *My thoughts and opinions are just as important as yours so if you want me to listen then you need to listen to me as well. Can you do that?*
- *That hasn't been my experience.*
- *Let's agree to disagree*
- *I'm embarrassed that you brought that up in front of everyone. Please talk about this topic in private with me next time.*
- *I'm overwhelmed right now so it's difficult for me to focus on feedback. I need a break.*

Equally, I think a bunch of the General Social Scripts are useful here too because if you're talking about trauma or why you don't want to go out and do something. Then you can simply say *I don't have to explain myself to you.* Even though I have to admit because of my trauma that is a really scary idea.

Social Scripts For Safety

For a lot of trauma survivors, safety is a very weird concept because I do feel a lot safer than I used to and I truly understand in my head what safety is, but I don't always feel it. There are only certain situations I feel truly safe in and that no one will hurt me at all, even though I have never actually been physically hurt. There was always the threat because I'm gay but emotional safety is important too. Something I have never really had.

Therefore, you might not feel physically or emotionally safe when you're with your family so you might need to establish boundaries to secure your safety and the safety of other people.

Some Safety Social Scripts can include:

- *I'm not attending that family event if This Person is going.*
- *I'm happy to come but I will not be left alone with This Person.*

- *Whenever I visit you always invalidate me so I feel hurt and unsupported. If you want me to continue visiting hen you need to stop invalidating me.*
- *I'm happy to spend time with you but it has to be outdoors, not indoors.*
- *I know you can take me but I want to drive there myself. That way I can leave when I need to.*
- *No thank you, I don't want to be touched.*

Personally, this is a category I'm going to be focusing on for my own conversations because social stuff is all about safety and I want to feel more comfortable doing social things with my "social environment". Instead of them always invalidating me, my rape and my trauma. As well as I need to get so much better at reinforcing my no-touch-without-permission rule because last time my "social environment" did that, it was bad. And it's an awful example of how my childhood trauma comes up so I'm too scared to reinforce my boundaries.

Social Scripts To Use About Children

Whilst I really want to have children in the future, I don't have any children at the moment. However, a caregiver's main job is to ensure their child is safe and they have good welfare so your family members might or might not be biologically related to your child, they may or may not be close or expect to be in charge of your child. Yet ultimately, these family members are not responsible for your child.

You are.

As a result, it's up to you to set any boundaries you deem necessary to take care of your child.

Some Social Scripts About Children Include:

- *Do not use those words in front of my child.*
- *That (Specific Thing) is not up for debate when it comes to my child.*
- *As their caregiver, I made the final decision because I am responsible for their welfare and wellbeing.*
- *Thanks for the feedback. I'll deal with it with (other parent or child) and I'll reach out if I need extra feedback.*
- *You can ask my child if they want to hug you but please don't force them. Respect their physical boundaries.*

Conclusion

As a survivor myself of two types of trauma, I understand how scary this is. The idea of setting boundaries with my family that I need to reinforce after 22 years, absolutely terrifies me because it is so new, unknown and I know I am going to be met with so much resistance. Yet I know this is critical to my mental health going forward and I cannot heal from my trauma and my rape without these boundaries being reinforced so it's hard.

Just please give yourself a chance to make these boundaries, enforce them and start to heal. You deserve to have a healthy relationship with your family, regardless of how impossible, scary and intimidating it may seem.

START OF AN EATING DISORDER, FEEL THE FEAR BUT EMBRACE, DISCOVER WHO YOU ARE: LESSONS FROM A FOURTH SESSION

I need to start off this chapter by apologising and being even more honest than I am in the rest of the book. Since normally at the end of each therapy session or in the next few days afterwards, I write an email draft with what we covered, some lessons learnt and other useful things that will help me write out these chapters.

That did not happen whatsoever for the third session of my rape counselling.

Whilst I cannot be sure of the reason why because that was around 9 weeks ago, it was probably because for the first four or five specialist counselling sessions, they were really hard on me. I would come home from counselling and later that evening I would have a complete and utter mental health crisis because it was so hard for me to process, calm down and my counsellor did say at least one wrong thing a session.

This chapter really proves that.

Looking back I think these crises were because I was struggling so much with my mental health anyway that it wasn't massively difficult to say the wrong thing. Therefore, I think it was the stress of dealing with my PTSD, other trauma responses and something she said that made me just not have the mental capacity or even remember to write down anything useful that week.

That's why there are no reflections or lessons from my third session.

The "Start" of An Eating Disorder

Personally, I cannot really say that my eating disorder (anorexia) started around the time of my third counselling session, because I have always struggled with eating in recent years. I was clinically obese as a young teenager so of course, I got bullied for that a lot at school, scouts and everywhere I went I was bullied for it. Thankfully, I managed to drop down to an average weight during the middle and late parts of my adolescence, but I later developed problematic eating.

During my first year of undergrad in 2019/2020, I lived on campus accommodation because without realising it, I was eating barely 1,000 calories a day without thinking about it. I simply didn't want to put on any weight and I was fine. Sure, I was very fatigued around 5 pm every night but I didn't see that as a problem.

Then in March 2020, COVID-19 hit and I went home to my parents, started eating normally again and I put on all the weight I had dramatically loss.

That's the historical context but the issue I had in 2024 was that my rapist was a very fat man. He was massive and that was a God's sent in a way because it meant his dick didn't work properly which is something I will always, always be grateful for. Yet it quickly became apparent that I was terrified of fat men because it reminded me too much of my rapist and I was obsessed with the idea of making sure I reached 10,000 steps a day for a whole month directly after my rape.

I did not want to gain any weight under any circumstances.

Leading us to the present situation and my fourth counselling session.

Around the time of my fourth session, me and my housemates had noticed that I was eating less and less. I was barely hitting a 1,000 calories a day and I had been losing a kilogram a week. Therefore, my best friend highly suggested that I mention my eating to my counsellor so we could work on it as it is a trauma response.

That did not go down well.

Note: as with everything in this book, these are only my experiences with my rape and with my counsellor. You should always talk to your counsellor about anything you want because the majority of the time they will know exactly what to do or they will least listen to you and signpost you to the correct service or support.

I mentioned to my counsellor that I have my eating disorder, I eat a lot less than I should and I think this is linked to my rape because he was a massive fat guy and I never want to end up like him.

She denied I had an eating disorder and she said that I was okay. She stressed that if I wanted to lose weight then I need to own it and do it for me, not because of my rape. As well as we explore my past eating and found that it was based in my childhood trauma of bullying over my weight then my rape had simply magnified that trauma and pain.

In all fair, my rape trauma had magnified a lot of my past trauma. Especially considering how I had to survive, cope and I want to say constantly fight in my childhood as I dealt with a family that hated gay people, and a social world that didn't understand me because of my undiagnosed autism.

In addition, I mentioned to my counsellor that another driving force behind my lack of eating was my ideas about wanting to be attractive. I wanted to lose weight so I could be more attractive so I could possibly find a partner and for someone to love me for the first time. Then maybe if I lose weight I could find someone who would actually like me for me and not rape me.

A slightly unhealthy view of attraction.

Therefore, my counsellor helped me to understand that "attraction does what attraction does". In other words, she helped me to understand that weight doesn't determine attraction because two people can be attracted to each other through more than weight.

If two people are attracted to each other then that attraction will be there regardless of weight. So I don't need to worry about my weight being linked to my attractiveness because that isn't how it works in the real world.

I will note that at the time of writing, my eating disorder has gotten a lot worse and I am showing more signs of anorexia than ever before, and eating is becoming a lot more difficult. I even went to the GP (doctor's) about my eating disorder but the GP and the counsellor both said I was fine because I haven't lost *enough* weight to be treated. The doctor put me in for a blood test but I passed the blood test so medically I am fine and I need to get a lot, lot worse before I can be helped.

Personally, I am completely fine with that but my best friend and my other housemates are getting really worried about my weight loss and my eating. They want me to find a therapist this week and I will but I just don't want to get told yet again that I am fine when I am really not.

Anyway that might be a future topic of a future book perhaps.

Camouflaging, Finding Out Who You Are And

Feel The Fear But Do it Anyway

Building upon the eating disorder section of the session, we spoke about camouflaging and how I need to try to cut down on it. Now camouflaging is the term she used to describe how I pretend that I am perfectly okay, I ignore my emotions and I act like nothing is wrong when the opposite is the case.

She helped me to understand how I've been camouflaging my entire life and she is right, too right actually. I camouflaged my entire adolescence, I had to hide and mask the fact that I was gay with such fierce devotion and commitment that I didn't know who I was anymore. The same goes for my autism, I had to mask and fight and study others with such intensity just to survive and function in a world that did not want me to be autistic. That was largely a mixture of friends and family but it was a constant fight just to survive.

And of course, I wasn't always successful so I was bullied, mocked and people thought I was a creep at times. All because they didn't know I was autistic and didn't understand how I struggled with the basic social graces that they took for granted so easily.

Back when I had my mental breakdown in August 2023 and I had my counselling back then, I mentioned how I didn't know who I was anymore because all I know is how to survive and fight. I don't know how to live, I don't know how to relax and I don't know how to live.

Or even be at peace.

All I knew how to do was camouflage my emotions so I could survive. Hell, it was exactly what I did the night I was raped. I just wanted, needed to survive.

And that's what I did. I survived.

Therefore, my counsellor explained to me how learning to uncamouflage involves me listening to my body, paying attention to my anxiety and everything that my body and mind is trying to tell me. Then if I need to leave or change something or ask for something to help me cope then that's what I need to do.

It was a hard conversation to have because all I know is camouflaging so identifying it was going to be impossible. Yet she mentioned how I need to start finding out who *I* am and that I need to make sure I am not scared to find out, because once I know who I am then it will help me to camouflage less.

Instead of camouflaging to survive by making my decisions based on what will help me to survive. I can make more decisions based on who I am, what my values are and how I am feeling in a given moment.

Decision making is about surviving, it is about doing what's best for me and up until that counselling session I had never really thought about it like that before.

And I'm grateful for that lesson. Actually am, I haven't really thought about that lesson much in the past 9 weeks but given how much better I've been doing and the sorts of decisions I've been making, I've been doing it.

And whilst my counsellor really messed up with the eating disorder conversation so badly that it's negatively impacting me now, she did teach me a great lesson that session.

That's a win and in counselling and in the early stages of trauma recovery, you really have to take all the wins you can.

Thankfully, this was a great win to have.

HOW TO SURVIVE A MAJOR DEPRESSIVE EPISODE?

From our clinical psychology lectures, watching the media and talking to friends and peers at university or in the workplace, we know that depression is serious and can even be life-threatening. Depression can lead to increases in self-harm, suicidal ideation and it can be crippling. Therefore, it's important to know how to survive a major depressive episode. Even if you don't have depression yourself, this is still a useful chapter that will give you a lot of useful ideas and unofficial tips and techniques to help someone in the future. And if you are depressed then this chapter will give you a lot of ideas to think about for the future.

Why Is Depression Serious And Potentially Life-Threatening?

Before we talk about the five main ways how you or a client can survive a major depressive episode, I want to remind people how serious Depression is and how dangerous it can be. Granted, I was reminded of this yesterday because even though I'm not clinically depressed, there have been two times in the past 6-months where I've been so depressed I simply couldn't move. There were other consequences too but I want to keep this chapter light as always.

Therefore, depression is the leading cause of disability in the world according to Friedrich (2017) as well as about 34% of people with bipolar disorder and about 31% of people with major depression disorder will attempt suicide in their lifetime (Dong et al., 2019; Dong et al., 2020). On the whole, when we add those percentages to the fact that depression is most associated with suicide, it makes us realise that depression can be life-threatening.

Hence, why we need to think about and make it common knowledge about how to survive a major depressive episode.

In addition, major or severe depression can be linked at times to changes in a person's information and sensory integration. This is called Psychosis, and this type of psychosis tends to take on a dark, depressive-congruent quality. For instance, a person experiencing this type of psychosis might experience persecutory delusions so they truly believe that the people around them are trying to harm them and they hate them or they can hear unkind voices too. Interestingly, about 10% of people with major depressive disorder (Dold et al., 2019) as well as 63% of people with bipolar disorder experience psychotic features (Aminioff et al., 2022).

Overall, I know you're all psychology students, professionals and people interested in psychology here, but we absolutely cannot underestimate depression. That is half the problem I think is the world at times, because we hear ignorant people saying they're "depressed" about the weather or that their football team is losing and they actually don't understand what their talking about. Instead they are just using a word with a critical, vital meaning outside of a clinical context and this doesn't help our clients. This only waters down the meaning of an important term so people don't think depression is as important as it is and this stops people from seeking help when they need it and it creates extra barriers for our clients too.

Thankfully, it's important to note that people can recover from depression regardless of its severity, and there are more treatments than ever before to help people. I've spoken about them in podcast episodes before and in my books, with different forms of psychotherapy and anti-depressants being first-line treatments.

How To Survive A Major Depressive Episode?

It Will Not Always Be This Way

I have to admit that when you are going through a major depressive episode, you seriously don't remember this and I always forget it. I don't remember that this is a temporary thing and I think this is how my life will be from now on because in the moment or the hours or day that it lasts, this is how my life seems.

And it doesn't help that when you are healthy again, the experiences of depression just feel so disconnected from you because it feels completely foreign.

Therefore, it's good to remind ourselves and our clients that the vast majority of major depressive episodes are temporary, as well as even with the longer-lasting depression episodes, there are usually moments of happiness.

If your client is in a major depressive episode, remember that this is temporary and there will be moments of happiness again.

Sometimes it can help to look over pictures and other memories from times when you were happy. Also when your client is healthy again, get them to write a note of encouragement to remind themselves of these times when they don't feel happy.

Depression never lasts.

Seek Meaning

This is an interesting one because even when a person is in a depressive episode, they can normally find meaning in small things or they can take steps towards their values. Since depression is an oppressive force so clients might want to find out what they can do and look for opportunities to live how you see as meaningful.

Yesterday, I was sort of reminded of this because at my university, I want to reform the Psychology Society and I had emailed a final-year student on the 1st of May and she replied the same night. It was the 24th of May yesterday and I still hadn't replied and I noticed her and a group of people had tried to message me on Teams. So I forced myself to go onto my laptop and look at what had happened in the email and on Teams. It was a nice reminder that people wanted to talk to me, be with me and work with me for the long term. And I seriously do want to start up the psychology society again and be President.

Equally, I had a specialist appointment at the university again on Monday and this is basically what the woman said. She stressed that I should do a lot of self-care, throw myself into my interests and stick to my values and what would bring me joy.

Ask For Help

Last night me and a friend went to go and play Tennis because my friend was probably a little worried about me, and when we got back to their place, we were talking. I still hate their kitchen. I know it's a student house but I hate their kitchen with a passion and I'm also glad the house we're moving into together has a nice kitchen.

Anyway, we were talking about mental health and my friend said that based on their experience, they realised that when it comes to mental health you never really notice how bad of a place you were in until you look back later on. I largely agree with the comment and depression is very good at hiding that from you. This touches on a different topic altogether.

However, my point is that when you realise you need help, it's okay to ask for it.

If you haven't received mental health support before then contact different services, find a therapist by searching for it online or ask for help in other ways. Just make sure you get the professional help you.

If you're already in therapy or getting another form of mental health support then asking for help means asking for more or different help than what you're currently getting. This is something I'm struggling with at the moment because my normal therapist was brilliant for helping me with my child abuse and trauma. She isn't so good at helping me now, which isn't her fault because sexual violence work is so specialised at times so I reached out to charity and I have a counselling assessment next Friday.

Additionally, if there's a risk you or your client is at risk of self-harming or suicide then reach out to crisis services like the 988 suicide prevention lifeline. Also, a therapist and even a primary care doctor can help you.

When it comes to asking for help, you can also reach out to your natural support systems like your family and friends too.

In addition, one of the most annoying feelings in the world is when you don't feel like you're able to get help straight away or you're told "no" in different ways. For example, I hate it when my therapist doesn't have an appointment for me for a week and a bit, that is just annoying because I want support now and I'm not able to get it. Another form of this is when clients are looking for inpatient programmes and the programmes they want to get into don't have any "beds" available.

When this happens, you need to keep trying and realise that you reaching out for support is an act of defiance against your depression, so keep doing it. Keep looking for therapists, support and other options.

Just please make sure you get the help and support you need.

<u>Remember Your Reasons For Living</u>

I know from personal experience how extremely difficult this can be during a depressive episode.

When it comes to reasons for living, a lot of people want to live so they can see their friends and family, they have hope for the future so they want to see what happens and they believe that they'll find something worth living for in the future. Yet during a depressive episode, it can seem like a client doesn't have any of these options and they can't even start to think of these things.

For example, being brutally honest about yesterday, I do have a good number to live for coming up. I have Summer Core at my university from mid-June to mid-July as a student ambassador so that's a lot of fun, really easy work with a great pay check attached. Me and my family are going to Kew Gardens somewhere I've always wanted to go, I'm going to Canterbury Pride with some friends and I'm moving in with my friends at the end of next month.

In addition, me having a lot of normal reasons to live for because my life is good.

I couldn't remember a single one of those reasons yesterday and even when I did remember, my depression or my mental health twisted it so these things didn't look like a reason to live.

As a result, when it comes to surviving a depressive episode, you need to remind yourself of reasons to live. You need to write down your reasons so you can read it and remember you have plenty of reasons to live for, as well as you can hang up pictures of the people that are close to you and love you too.

Just give yourself as many reminders that life is worth living as possible.

Conclusion

I never really intended to do a chapter on depression but I wasn't really inspired or bothered about any of the other topics I have on my list after what happened yesterday. And I have to admit that I like chapters like this because even though nothing in this book is official advice, I still like that I can do slightly more practical and applied chapters that will hopefully help a student, professional or another person entirely.

Going through a depressive episode is awful and I don't wish it on anyone, but there is always hope and you are never alone.

There is always support available and whilst it might seem difficult to find, it is there and there are lots of people happy and ready to help you, because you deserve it.

You never deserve to suffer in silence and you can survive a major depressive episode.

You seriously can.

WHAT TO DO WHEN DEPRESSION MAKES IT IMPOSSIBLE TO GET OUT OF BED?

I wanted to include this next chapter because during the worse of my mental health because of my rape, it was very typical for me to take hours upon hours to get out of bed in the morning. For me, getting out of bed felt like it would take way too much energy and it feels impossible.

This was awful, scary and it made me feel even worse about myself. I felt useless, pathetic and I meant I was laying in bed with nothing to do except ruminate about my sexual trauma even more, leading to me trauma responses. Over time, this only created an evil cycle of me not being able to get out of bed so I thought rape and I experienced more trauma responses, so it felt even more impossible to get out of bed and so on.

As a result, I wanted to include this next chapter to help you understand this consequence of sexual trauma and how might be able to support yourself if you encounter this difficulty.

Of course, whilst nothing in this book is any form of official advice, this will hopefully still be very interest, useful and insightful.

Enjoy.

***

With depression being one of the most common mental health conditions in the world, a lot of a clinical psychologist's workload will be supporting people with depression. A common depression symptom is what's known as "Leaden Paralysis" and one of the effects of the symptoms is that everyday tasks take a million times more energy to complete. This can make the "simple" task of getting out of bed feel impossible for people with depression. Therefore, in this chapter, you'll learn what is leaden paralysis, why leaden paralysis impacts people's mental health and what to do when depression makes it impossible to get out of bed.

What is The Weight of Depression?

If you've ever experienced depression then you might be aware that there are some days where your depression will weigh you down so much that it feels like your body is made of lead and concrete. This makes the very notion of doing anything, much less leave your bed feel flat out impossible. As well as the sheer weight of depression might make you cancel plans, spend more time at home and/ or you might miss or be late for work.

This weight of depression and a struggle to get out of bed can take a massive toll on your work, relationships and your quality of life.

Personally, during August until October 2024 when I had quite severe depression, it always took me about two hours to get out of bed in the morning. Getting out of bed just felt hard because I had fun things to do, I could see my friends and everything but it wasn't good enough motivation to actually want to get out of bed. I just wanted the day to be over so I could sleep and I didn't have to deal with all the trauma responses that I was having every single hour of every single day.

What Is Leaden Paralysis?

As a result, there is a symptom of depression called "leaden paralysis" that causes people with depression to experience a severe drop in energy and as Qi et al. (2020) highlights this makes everyday tasks a million times harder for the individual. This is important to bear in mind because a lot of people who have never experienced depression or severe depression before might argue that people should just get up. Yet it isn't that easy. And this is one of the reasons why depression is a leading cause of disability round the world (Friedrich, 2017).

One of the clearest examples for me of leaden paralysis was on the very first day of my severe depression when it took me 5 hours just to have a shower. After struggling to get up for two or three hours, I managed to eventually make breakfast and at midday I decided to try to have a shower. Yet everything felt so heavy, I was so drained, I had no energy and my body might as well have had 20kg kettlebells tied to it.

It took so long to go through the living room, up the stairs, grab my towel and clothes, go across the landing, go into the bathroom, undressed, etc, etc.

Every one of those steps felt so impossible and each one took so long.

That is what leaden paralysis is like and that's why supporting people with depression is so important. You can probably imagine but having leaden paralysis doesn't make you feel great and it can make you feel even worse about yourself as your quality of life starts to crumble, so this is why mental health support is critical.

What To Do When Depression Makes It Impossible To Get Out Of Bed?

Here are three strategies to help people with depression overcome leaden paralysis and get out of bed in the mornings.

Firstly, you can break the day down into "hoops". This strategy involves breaking down your day into sections then you visualise these tasks as hoops. For example, getting up or brushing your teeth can be seen as two hoops that need to be conquered. After completing each task, you could imagine yourself jumping through each hoop and this can be an encouraging visual so you get a sense of achievement, and it helps to make the day less overwhelming. As well as on the really difficult days, seeing tasks as hoops can help you determine what tasks or hoops can be done on other days.

Secondly, you need to try to be kind to yourself because one of the ways how depression impacts us is makes us criticise ourselves more often. Therefore, to define your depression and how it criticizes you every chance it gets, you might want to practise self-kindness by using compassionate words when you realise your self-dialogue is getting more negative and harsher.

For example, today is actually a good example for me because my mental health definitely dipped today, and I was tired, overwhelmed and I was anxious about seeing my partner tomorrow because of trauma responses. My partner has done nothing wrong by the way. This meant I didn't get up for over an hour this morning and when I had a nap in the late afternoon in an effort to make myself feel better, I napped for 40 minutes but I didn't get out of bed for another two hours.

At first I was judging myself harshly because that was such a waste of time, I had so much to do and on and on and on. But I realised that it's okay I couldn't get out of bed earlier because this is what happens when my mental health dips. I need to listen to myself, figure out what's causing my mental health to dip and just keep going. Things will get better later on or tomorrow and as long as I focus on just going forward then that's okay. As well as I am hardly alone because this happens to everyone at different times in their life, even more so when you have depression and other mental health difficulties.

This is what works for me, you might need other self-compassionate and self-kindness thoughts.

The key is to not feed into your depression by criticising and hating yourself because you can't get out of bed. This will only make it feel even harder to do everyday tasks.

Finally, reach out for mental health support, because if you're experiencing depression that is so severe you find it really difficult to get out of bed. It is important that you seek mental health support as soon as possible because if you don't get support then your symptoms might get worse and your risk of suicide and self-harm increase. I really don't want that for you. As well as your depression might make you want to be alone and isolate yourself, but when you're struggling, it is a really good idea to be surrounded by other people. These people can include friends and family, but make sure you reach out to mental health professionals like a therapist or a mental health helpline too. Since if you isolate yourself then you might quickly find yourself in an echo chamber surrounded by your negative thoughts and inactivity and this will only maintain your depression.

And make you feel worse and worse until you don't see another way out.

Whenever I go through depression and mental health difficulties, reaching out to mental health support is always the best thing

I could have done. It is always nerve-racking, I try to put it off as long as possible and I try to deal with things on my own at first. Yet ultimately seeing a counsellor, therapist or another form of mental health support is always best and I grow and develop so much and I flat out love the process too.

Conclusion

Whether you're an aspiring or qualified psychologist or person with depression, we've learnt a lot in this chapter. For psychologists, a lot of our future work will be with people with depression and we will encounter leaden paralysis the majority of the time because it is a common symptom. I know as someone who has experienced the inability to get out of bed frequently in the past, this is very distressing, it makes you feel awful about yourself and it can play into suicidal thoughts. Especially, when every single other everyday task seems to require so much effort that your quality of life just crumbles and is reduced to nothing.

This is why learning about strategies to support clients with leaden paralysis is so important.

For people with depression, I hope you now have some strategies to help you get out of bed in the morning and I hope you realise that you aren't alone. What you're experiencing is normal for depression and it is a normal response for whatever is causing your difficulties and that's why talking to a mental health professional is critical.

Here are some questions at the end of this chapter:

- Have you ever encountered leaden paralysis before? Either through personal or clinical experience.
- How have you dealt with these experiences of leaden paralysis?
- Do you know how to practise self-kindness?
- How could you learn more about self-kindness?
- What would you say to a loved one and/ or client who struggles to get out of bed in the morning because of their depression?

SOMETIMES IT GETS WORSE BEFORE IT GETS BETTER: LESSONS FROM FIFTH SESSION OF RAPE COUNSELLING

Around the time of my 5th counselling session, my mental health was really taking a turn for the worse because at this point, the rape counselling wasn't helping as much as I needed. I didn't feel like it was working, I felt my counsellor was always saying the wrong thing and my PTSD was getting worse and worse.

So, this is really hard to write but I want you to know dear reader that a lot of the so-called "dark" or "negative" trauma responses that happen to a rape survivor are normal reactions to an extremely abnormal situation. As well as I want you to see over the course of this book that my mental health has dramatically improved and my PTSD, anxiety and all my other trauma responses have basically gone at the time of writing (week 11).

Yet I tried to kill myself that week.

It's 8 weeks ago so I don't really remember it clearly but I just remember that my best friend was helping one of our housemates Ruby (a fake name) because their mental health wasn't the best that night. Then me and my other housemate were simply sitting on the two sofas just talking and I felt so bad I just started scratching my wrist.

I kept going until it was painful and then I realised my best friend (yes, not me) was going to get really stressed about this and it was going to impact them badly. So I went upstairs and grabbed a plaster and stuff and the night got worse and worse for me, I was getting more and more suicidal but I didn't try again too much.

Then my best friend had a long conversation with me because they were scared that I hadn't called them, they explained how me dying would ruin their life and they care about a lot. I already knew all this but it was nice to hear it again I suppose.

My mental health was still horrific for another week.

In addition, as part of our conversation, me and my best friend spoke about how we need to continue to plan fun things together so I have something to look forward to. This is why even now we schedule time together every Tuesday and Sunday. For example, last Sunday we went to see Wicked: Part One and we went to a Vietnamese restaurant in Canterbury. It was a lovely six hours together.

Moreover, they made me write down the following on a Note on my phone:

"No I'm not a burden. They're my friend

No we don't only talk about my mental health. Then List other stuff we talk about

IT WILL RUIN THEIR LIFE IF I KILL MYSELF"

You can see one of the reasons why I was suicidal in that note. I just felt like all we were talking about was my mental health and it wasn't a good friendship anymore, because I felt like my best friend was a carer and not a friend. As well as because I felt like all we were doing was talking about my mental health was I felt like a massive burden.

That's why I tried to kill myself that night and thankfully I didn't, because life is really good now and you'll see that in the future chapters.

NEVER KILL YOURSELF.

Furthermore, me and my best friend spoke about me looking into my savings or asking my parents for money for a therapist, because at that point in time, my rape counselling just wasn't having much of an effect on me. At least not a positive effect.

PowerPoint Night

Then two days later on the Tuesday, I had another mental health crisis as did Ruby, because we went to Neurodivergent Society PowerPoint presentation night at my university. Basically, a bunch of autistic and ADHD people give a 20-minute max presentation about their special interest (something they are REALLY passionate about).

Someone was interested in witchcraft and spells and the Society committee hadn't thought to check exactly what content was covered in the PowerPoint. The witchcraft one covered a lot of non-consensual love spells and erotic-binding spells.

My mind went mad at that so when I got back with my housemates I had a full-on mental health crisis because non-consensual stuff was so triggering for me.

It was so bad that I sent the following message to the President of the Society:

"Hey thanks for doing the presentation

night earlier and letting me present. It was great to see the other presenters, but could the society please screen the PowerPoints first for trigger warnings?

Because the first presentation mentioned a lot of non-consent and erotic-binding spells. It was a great topic but considering I was raped a few months ago, I find non-consent sex and romance extremely triggering. And I had full on mental health crisis when I got back.

Please know I'm not blaming the presenter, the society or anyone else. It's just a trigger warning would have been nice. I'm probably just as guilty even referencing trans mental health."

I got a very supportive message back and I was surprised that the very next day, the society started advertising for two welfare officers. One of them became my best friend so it all worked out in the end but it was an extremely rough night.

<u>My Fifth Counselling Session</u>

Now that you know the context behind my fifth counselling session, we can move onto the session itself and it did not go well. I should mention here that it takes a lot of courage to actually go to counselling or therapy in the first place because you aren't sure if it's going to work, you have to reveal personal details to someone who is effectively a stranger and it is a tense time. Especially after sexual violence, but I always recommend therapy and counselling because mental health professionals do have the skills to help decrease your distress, improve your lives and give you new adaptive coping mechanisms.

It takes even more courage to tell a counsellor that you tried to kill yourself.

That's what I did and it didn't go well.

She seemed concerned (clearly) but there was a judgmental undertone and her voice sounded angry. I'm not sure if it actually was but she wasn't happy and her words only confirmed it. "Well Connor, that's a big statement to make,"

I've been a psychology student, podcaster and I've read more than enough about therapy to know what her response should have been. So I felt scared and nervous so whilst I should have challenged her, I didn't.

I explain a lot more in the next chapter about how a mental health professional should respond to a suicide revelation. She helped me to explore what led to the suicide attempt and why I felt like that was the only way out.

I didn't really want to talk to her too much after her reaction but I was there for counselling and I was there for psychological support, so I was going to talk for the sake of it.

She helped me learn 3 things that I could take away by the end of the session (but when I made more dramatic attempts on my life 5 days later, I didn't tell her. something I seriously do not recommend for you to do).

You'll see in the next therapy chapter how I had a major breakthrough but that's not the focus of this chapter.

Anyway, she helped me to understand that I need to allow myself to feel what I need and want to feel. Since the event that started the chain of events that led to my suicide attempt was 2 days before the attempt on the Friday, I had a meeting with a friend of mine who's doing his PhD and he works at my university's Parkinson's clinic. He had spoken to the clinical psychologist at the clinic who I had been talking about my PhD idea with, and he had some news to give me.

He said that the clinical psychologist (who is the national leading expert on Brief Psychological Interventions) said that my idea for a Brief psychological Intervention for rape survivors wasn't practical. Since it wouldn't get through ethics because it could be unethical to give rape survivors some mental health support that has an end date and ethics wouldn't allow me to do clinical work with such a vulnerable group. As well as she wasn't sure that Brief Psychological Interventions would be useful for rape survivors because they need a lot more support than BPIs are designed to give. Finally, she didn't think the project was practical because it would require someone at the university to be clinically trained and able to clinically supervise me.

She would have liked to but her contract didn't allow it.

The issue with this rejection of my PhD proposal was that I didn't allow myself to grieve. This was an idea I was extremely excited by because I knew this had the potential to stop so, so many rape survivors from going through what I went through over the summer.

I knew I felt grief, I was upset and I was really devastated that I wasn't able to do this amazing project. My error was that I didn't allow myself to feel these emotions because I knew they were going to hurt so I simply let them build and build and build along with everything else going on in my life.

In addition, she encouraged me to use the Three Good Things technique from positive psychology and even now I still do this because it is a great technique that helps you to understand and appreciate that even on the darkest days, there are good things to celebrate.

Below is an extract from a psychology article I wrote that explains what this technique is:

<u>"What Is The Three Good Things Techniques?</u>

Interestingly enough I learnt our next technique when I was talking to a Final Year undergraduate student one afternoon when we were both sitting in a psychology area that only researchers have access to. She had my older placement and Final Year Project supervisor as her own so we were talking about her project.

She mentioned one of her experiments that her group was working on was using this next technique in a two-week intervention to improve depressed mood.

That was my first encounter with technique and it's interested me ever since, and it's appeared back in my life again recently as I still reel from my trauma and mental health.

As a result, the Three Good Things technique was introduced in 2005 by Martin Seligman for clients with low self-esteem and/ or depressed mood so they could do this in 5 or 10 minutes a day. The technique involves a client writing down three positive things that happened that day. Also, what's really good about this technique is that even on the roughest of days, there will be some positives as well as these positives don't have to be great.

For example, my mental health was truly, truly horrific last Tuesday at the time of writing, but my positive things would still be:

- I allowed myself to hug my dear friend so they touched me.
- I gave a presentation at neurodivergent society.
- I brought myself some Biscoff chocolate.

You can see in this example, there are two "big" positives and a small one and that's okay.

If we look at the next day, which was another bad day. There are no "big" positives but there were still positives in the day.

- I got up to go to counselling as much as I didn't want.
- I saw my parents.
- I brought back supplies Dad had brought me from Costco.

Therefore, whilst there were no "big" positives in that list. It was still really nice seeing my parents, seeing that Dad brought me a lot of Tassimo pods for my machine and I went to counselling.

We all need to take the wins and this technique helps you to realise that there are always positives in your life. No matter how dark the world seems.

Moreover, the advantage of this technique is that it encourages clients to be positive and it improves their mood. Yet these three good things can feel forced or artificial at times.

Lastly for this technique, my counsellor just calls this technique "adding some positive psychology" into your life. Now, I am have major issues with her calling the technique that because positive psychology is an entire massive discipline, you cannot put an entire discipline into your life. But she recommends I start using the technique so I can focus on the positives and this is something I seriously need to start doing.

Maybe we all do."

Ultimately, whilst I didn't like how she responded to my revelation that I tried to kill myself because it was judgmental and there wasn't the level of support in terms of empathy and compassion that I needed in that moment. I still learnt some important things like the Three Good Things technique that still benefits my mental health even now.

Yes. Sometimes your mental health will get worse before it gets better but counselling and social support are always useful for helping you get through it.

HOW SHOULD THERAPISTS REACT AFTER A SUICIDE REVELATION?

In the last chapter, I mentioned how I don't feel like my counsellor handled my suicide revelation very well so I wanted to investigate how therapists and other mental health professionals *should* handle this revelation. Since I understand that this might be the worst case scenario for any aspiring or even qualified psychologist, because when their client reveals they want to or they have attempted suicide. This naturally feels any psychologist with dread and fear because this is a very serious situation.

That's why I've added in this chapter adapted from a podcast episode because it is ultimately, a therapist's words, actions and body language to a suicide revelation that determines what happens next. Since if they react negatively then this can make the client feel invalidated, silly and stupid so this makes them more distant and disengaged in therapy. Also, it harms the therapeutic alliance as well as if a client feels alienated from their therapist (the one person in the world who is meant to support them, help them and be there for them) then the darker option can be a lot, lot more tempting. On the other hand, if a client feels supported by their therapist's "positive" reaction to their revelation then this can deepen trust and ultimately allow the therapist to get through to the client to help them heal in a very dark time in their life. Therefore, in this chapter, you'll learn how therapists should react to a suicide revelation and some tips and techniques to help therapists in this situation. If you enjoy learning about mental health, suicide and clinical psychology then this will be a great chapter for you.

Why Am I Talking About This Topic?

For context and as much as I don't want to admit it, I did do a suicide attempt in mid-October 2024 and it was a hellish night for me. As well as my best friend when they eventually found out about it. Granted a lot happened that night for other people and it gave me the shock that I needed to know I had to start looking after myself better because what I was currently doing wasn't enough, even though I thought it was.

Therefore, after a rough Tuesday night and Wednesday morning, I had specialist counselling on Wednesday at 12 pm. I told my therapist that I attempted suicide but I really didn't like her reaction. I wanted or imagined a therapist to clearly be shocked, concerned and maybe even scared internally. Yet externally, I wanted her to take a deep breath and simply say something along the lines of this, *Okay, firstly, thank you for telling me. I know that couldn't have been easy but I'm glad you told me. Secondly, you know this is serious so, can you please tell me what happened?*

A therapist is meant to be non-judgmental and 100% supportive in this situation. Yet my counsellor wasn't and she messed up with me because her first thing was "Well Connor, that's a massive statement you made. You tried to commit suicide," and I didn't like her tone or her facial expressions because they were not non-judgemental.

And because her tone was slightly angry, I did disengage. I went into flight-freeze-fight in her therapy room for a little bit. And I calmed down as we spoke about what happened, what led up to the event but even now I am not okay because of some of the things she said during this conversation.

For example, she accused me of playing games with myself because I keep trying to do small distressing things when I can't. Instead I would have preferred her to say something kinder. Maybe something like "Do you think it's a pattern that your PTSD gets triggered by, in your own words, *small* things?" then I would like to imagine this would start a conversation getting *me* to realise that I need to just leave as soon as I get distressed so I can handle the little things.

Anyway, that's a topic for another day.

Ultimately, my counsellor made me feel bad, unsupported and very judged at a time when I seriously did not need to be judged. Therefore, I wanted to learn about how therapists should react to suicide revelations and whilst the rest of the chapter isn't an exhaustive and ultimate guide. It will surely help you be a million times better than my counsellor.

Let's begin.

How Should Therapists React To A Suicide Revelation?

In the rest of the chapter, we're going to look at 7 points explaining how therapists should respond to clients with suicidal thoughts. Yet when it comes to each of these points, it is critical to remember that clients must be treated with empathy, compassion and professionalism. These three things are the most important aspects of this situation.

You Need To Actively and Empathetically Listen To Suicidal Clients

Whenever you're faced with a suicidal client, you absolutely need to listen actively and empathetically because the client has decided to be extremely brave and tell you about this fact. The client will most probably be scared and utterly terrified that something bad will happen to them now. Sometimes they might be scared that you'll cart them off to a psychiatric ward, you'll prescribe them drugs or you will make them do something.

Whilst none of these fears are logical or based in reality in a general sense, the media, books and films have implanted these rare possibilities into our collective minds. Making these fears very real to our clients.

This is why our clients are extremely brave for telling us what's happening to them.

Therefore, it is important that you allow the client to express their feelings without any interruption as well as that you show empathy and you validate their emotions.

My counsellor tried to do this because she seemed angry at first, I interpreted them in my vulnerable state as judgment and invalidation. As well as I didn't feel like she was very empathetic to my reasons and my situation so I felt like she had put a wedge between us. This isn't what you want with clients.

You Need To Assess The Risk

There are a lot of different tools and ways how you can do this and please stick to whatever your organisation uses, so I will talk more generally about this topic. Whenever you have a suicidal client, you seriously need to assess the risks because research shows that once a client tries to kill themselves, they are a lot more likely to have a suicide attempt and the last thing we want is for clients to keep trying and one day actually be successful.

This is a major area that my counsellor messed up in because she didn't do a risk assessment, she didn't do anything that I'm about to tell you and I honestly think even if she did I would have lied to her. Simply because she had put that wedge between us by making me feel judged and not understood. Since I first tried to kill myself three days before the appointment I told her in then there was her judgement and I tried to kill myself again 5 days later using two different methods.

Thankfully, I had a very healing day the following day so it will not happen again.

Anyway, a therapist or clinical psychologist should always carry out a thorough risk assessment to help you fully understand the severity of the suicidal idealisation within the client. It's useful to know about the duration, frequency and the intensity of the suicidal idealisation, and if there are any plans or means to carry out the suicide attempt.

My counsellor didn't ask me a single one of these basic questions.

You Need To Create A Safety Plan With Suicidal Clients

Professional training and different organisations have more detailed tips and guides about how to do this, but as a general overview, when a client reveals their suicidal idealisation, you need to create a safety plan with them. This is so the client has a guide or ideas about what to do instead of trying to commit suicide.

Therefore, in the development of this safety plan, you should include emergency contacts (like helplines), coping strategies so the client knows how to deal with suicidal thoughts and what steps they need to take if the suicidal thoughts get more intense and they want to make an attempt.

Again, my counsellor didn't do any of this kind of work with me and that was very dangerous. If she had calmly created a safety plan with me then things might have been different and I might not have tried again, so please make safety plans with your clients.

If The Client Agrees, Involve Support Systems

On the podcast and in my different rape-focused books, I've often spoken about how my best friend has been a major, major support system in my life since I was raped. My best friend has done a lot for me to ensure that I was safe, I was as okay as I could be and that I had hope for the future. We've spent a lot of time together, we've laughed a lot and we've created some really good memories together since I was raped.

Support systems are critical to everyone going through a mental health crisis.

As a result, if the client agrees, you can involve family members and the client's friends in the process so they can support the client. If this does happen, then the family members and friends need to understand the importance of their role in the client's safety. For example, they might be needed to sit with the client when you're suicidal, they might need to take away objects or do other things to prevent the client from killing themselves or they could do something else entirely.

The details change for every client and what their support system is like, but you get the general idea.

Therapists Should Provide Resources and Follow-Up To The Suicidal Client

Something else that my counsellor should have done as standard but she didn't was provide me with a list of resources. These resources are designed to help clients when they're suicidal and they need help the most. For example, these resources can and should include details of crisis hotlines, support groups and essentially anything that can help clients get immediate help.

This is something that will help the client when you're suffering the most and this could be the difference between an attempt and no attempt, let alone a successful or unsuccessful attempt.

The issue I had with my counsellor was that she didn't give me anything. I didn't know any hotlines, any ways to get additional help and I was just left still feeling a little suicidal after the appointment. My suicidality only got worse after that appointment.

Thankfully, I am okay now and I wouldn't do it again but at that time I was in so much pain.

Yet life gets better. I know that now.

In addition, therapists should follow up with suicidal clients by scheduling regular follow-up sessions to monitor their progress and adjust the intervention plan as needed.

Conclusion: Continue Your Professional Development

Once I was talking to a clinical psychologist who lectures at my university and he said something that I hope is going to stay with me. It doesn't matter what mental health service you work in, be it children and adolescents, eating disorders, depression or

Obsessive-Compulsive Disorder. Suicidality and suicide risk will always be on your workload at some point in your career, because this is the unfortunate reality of mental health and its negative consequences.

Therefore, I firmly believe that as part of your Continued Professional Development, you keep learning, investigating and researching about suicide prevention, and even postvention. It is critical for you as a therapist, and your clients, that you have the most updated knowledge and best practices about suicide prevention.

At some point in your career, you will meet and have to work with a suicidal client, and your training will matter more than ever. It's beyond critical for you to remain composed, calm and you are sure that clients feel heard and supported during this extremely difficult process. Hearing that a client is suicidal will be difficult for you and you will have an emotional reaction to such a revelation, but for the sake of the client, you need to remain calm and you need to focus on the client.

Make sure look yourself later on, use your clinical supervision to your benefit and make sure you don't get burnt out.

Yet ultimately, as a therapist, your response can and will make a significant difference to the client's journey towards recovery.

Your actions, your words, your response matters, so please keep learning, stay calm and remember to act with empathy and compassion. Two elements that are more important than ever.

GREAT HEALING MOMENT, A BRILLIANT SESSION. THINGS ARE LOOKING UP: LESSONS LEARNT FROM SESSION SIX

Everything in my life went to sh*t after my last therapy session and that is a large part of the first half of this chapter. I tried to kill myself in two very different ways but equally I had an extremely healing moment that I'll explain in a moment.

Now I will admit that I did not tell my counsellor about my two other suicide attempts after she reacted with such judgment without empathy or compassion, the last time that I made a revelation to her.

Therefore, in a moment, I'll explain what happened in the therapy session itself because there were a lot of major breakthroughs and I am extremely grateful that this therapy session happened.

Below is a long but fascinating extract from the conclusion of *I Am Not A Victim, I Am A Survivor* and I'm including it in the chapter, because you can see how happy I was the night it happened. Also, this was written the night before session 6 of my rape counselling.

It shows a lot of useful insights and lessons for sure.

Extract

"A Healing Moment is when something just snaps inside you and your entire world changes for the better. It does not mean you are "cured" (whatever that means and that isn't how mental health works anyway), it does not mean everything will be plain sailing anymore and it does not mean you will never be in pain again.

I am actually tearing up as I write this section.

A Healing Moment simply means you realise that there is hope that everything can get better, you are definitely not a victim and if everyone is telling you that life gets better (hopefully they are or they shouldn't be in your life) that you realise it and internalise it as the truth that it is.

In addition, Healing Moments look different for everyone and what mine looks like will probably be completely different to yours. Your Healing Moment might be tiny, yours might be massive, yours might make you cry or it might not.

It is *your* Healing Moment for a reason.

As a result, my Healing Moment happened today because I tried to kill myself twice last night in two different ways. I also found out I hurt my best friend by accident and I had done something wrong with a housemate that really hurt them. It was truly awful and I tried to kill myself.

Moreover, my mental health has been so bad for so long that I just couldn't see another way out. I've self-harmed, been suicidal for months and I have an eating disorder and on and on and on.

So I tried to kill myself.

Thankfully, my housemates subtly rallied around me and when I woke up this morning, I still felt suicidal but the idea of me hurting my best friend. Who I love romantically, who has always been there for me and the one person I have lived for for so long, I realised I had two choices.

Either I could keep trying to kill myself and ruin my best friend's life forever so I could find a new way of healing.

My best friend went to the gym with a new friend that I've made and getting close with, so I went into the library and started reading the *Healing Sexual Trauma Workbook* again. I have not read this book in months because I used to the possible "excuse" that my mental health was too bad that I didn't want to try it.

I had forgotten how great this book is for me personally. This book truly makes me feel understood and validated.

There was a simple exercise that changed everything.

The first chapter of the book focuses on feeling safe in your own skin and after the first few pages, the exercises focus on helping you to focus on the *feelings* of safety. For example, what does your body feel like when you feel unsafe then there's another question on what does your body feel like when you feel safe.

Those are not the actual wording of the questions and there are questions on thoughts during these times too, but you get the gist.

As a result, this is what I wrote for my answers:

When I feel unsafe, my body panics. My breathing increases but goes shallow, I shake and my thoughts go a million miles an hour.

When I feel safe, my body just feels 100% relaxed and untensed.

Now my counsellor has been wanting me to focus on my body for ages but maybe I was resistant to it, maybe I needed it to be worded differently, but that did not work for me.

However, me thinking and writing down how my body actually felt when I was safe was brilliant. It got me to label this feeling so I could savour it when I felt safe and I could focus on getting my body to that state.

In hindsight I did some weird stuff to

savour that feeling. I went and sat in two different toilets at the university and I went into a very busy Co-Op (just think corner shop on campus) and each time I focused on feeling completely relaxed and untensed. I savoured that wonderful feeling of being relaxed and my body just not caring or being in survival mode.

I am relaxed because I am safe. I am always safe.

Then of course, I felt depressed and bad for the next few hours because I felt awful about hurting my best friend. Granted, they had already forgotten about it at that point, but I read a bit more of the workbook.

I did some more exercises but I did something interesting. I focused on feeling 100% relaxed in my own home in Canterbury with my three housemates in the house.

I realised ever since mid-August when I had my mental health collapse and everything happened. I had not felt safe in this house, this has never been my home and I know I haven't enjoyed living with two extra housemates as much as I love them. In a way, I suppose I have never felt safe in this house either.

I 100% relaxed today in my own home and I could do it so easily.

And this is my home now. I belong in this house with my three housemates, I belong in Canterbury and I am not a problem and all the million other things my mind tries to tell me.

I am not a problem.

It is a lovely feeling to know that I am home.

Something else I've been struggling with lately was my best friend has been focusing a lot more on another housemate who is going through hell-and-back at the moment. Also, my best friend deals with us in extremely different ways and I think I have been a lot more jealous than I want to admit.

My mind has tried to twist it repeatedly as my best friend not liking me, hating me and my best friend not wanting to be friends anymore.

But the following message highlights a large part of my Healing Moment:

I'm really sorry I'm chronically insecure a lot of the time because you're all I have in terms of real support.

And that it's taken me so long to realise that you focusing more on, spending more time with and doing more tasks for R *isn't a reflection of you not liking, you hating me or our friendship breaking down so much so you're a carer, not a friend.*

Mine and R's mental health manifests in very different ways and you are more comfortable with them anyway. R needs the constant help and support right now and for the next few months, and that's okay. Because you've offered the same to me since June without me realising it and now you can't be in two places at once.

I need to focus on my healing for me and I know you are always there for me when I need it most, but now I need to take back control because otherwise something might genuinely happen to this friendship without even one of us seeing it until it's too late.

So what I'm saying is... Thank you for being the most amazing and patient friend I could ever ask for. And I understand what I need to do to heal now a little better.

You're still there for me and I am ALWAYS there for you and it will still hurt like hell at times for me because of my trauma, but I now realise I don't need you to make me feel safe in my own home.

And here with R, L *and especially you, you're all my home.*

(Yes I teared up writing this. I hope this makes sense and I don't come off as a dick)

Thankfully, my best friend found that message really cute and sweet, and I need to send one to R and L later (don't you just love how creative I am with pseudonyms).

Ultimately, my Healing Moment boiled down to finally, finally realising that I am worthy of people liking me for me. I don't need to think I'm a burden, I don't need to think unless I am a certain way I'll be safe and I don't need to rely on other people to make me feel safe, because I am safe. And as long as I focus on that 100% relaxed and untensed feeling in my body then I know, I will truly know that I am safe."

My Sixth Counselling Session

Overall, it was a brilliant session because it was the most positive session I had had up to that point, and it felt great that it was a session that focused on myself, what I needed and it celebrated the major success I had made that week.

It wasn't a session that made me feel bad, traumatised and it didn't make me feel hopeless. Granted, none of the sessions themselves ever made me feel like this, it was more the aftermath of the sessions and me still having to deal with PTSD, anxiety and other trauma responses.

That was not easy to still have to deal with after each of the other counselling sessions, but I actually didn't need to experience those things as much after this breakthrough and session.

In addition, during this session, I asked her about wanting to process more of the trauma instead of doing stabilisation work. In the next chapter, I explain more about the Trauma Recovery Model that my rape counselling is based on, at least, so you can understand how it works.

My counsellor mentioned how even when we're doing stabilisation work, I'm still processing the trauma and slowly integrating it into my everyday life. All three of those components are important parts of the Model that you'll look at next.

Personally, I really liked that explanation. Not only because she named the model so I could later research it on my own (granted it took me 9 weeks to research that model), but I liked knowing I was still making good progress. I liked processing what He had done to me that night and it was comforting to know that I wasn't "stuck" in the stabilisation stage, I was actually processing and progressing towards healing.

Ultimately, she explained how the aim of the specialist counselling as well as Recovery Model is to help me integrate the sense of safety into my life amongst a few other things so I can heal, thrive and live the life that I want to choose. In other words, I control my life, not my trauma.

3 Main Areas To Work On

The next part of the session really focused on the final stage of the trauma Recovery Model, focusing on integrating that sense of safety into your everyday life. I was really happy that we were focusing on this aspect because this is where I wanted to put my focus on now.

I wanted to focus on living, thriving and actually doing more than just surviving for the first time in my life. Therefore, we worked together to identify three major areas of my life that I wanted to focus on for now.

Dungeons And Dragons

Firstly, my best friend is in charge of a Dungeons and Dragons Campaign (DM) and they run this with our other housemates and some of our other friends. Amongst these other players with an overweight guy with longish brown hair (both of which are similar to my rapist) so being in the same room as him makes me very tense and over time it chips away at my mental health.

It was only a Friday or two before this sixth session that I just couldn't deal with DnD because my mental health just got too bad. Mainly because this player at no fault of their own was triggering my PTSD and other trauma responses too badly.

As a result, me and my counsellor discussed how I would in future use grounding techniques and focus on that physical feeling of safety to make DnD more manageable. Then over time as I get better at this skill and I'm able to desensitise myself further, I'll be able to stay in the room longer and longer.

Interestingly, I'm writing this chapter six weeks after this session and whilst I could argue that I have made no progress in this area because the triggering player hasn't joined us again (I doubt he will). I am actually going to celebrate how I have made a lot of progress in this area because the trigger I've been working on here is to do with fat men. In reality, my trauma responses are a lot better towards seeing, being in the same room and even being close to fat men.

Fat men no longer cause me to have trauma responses, experience intense anxiety or intrusive thoughts.

That is a major progress because I can go outside and live my life without being scared of my trauma responses around fat men.

<u>Going To The Gym</u>

Secondly, I really wanted to be able to go to the gym because it's something I can do with my friends, it's a way of seeing people and it means I can keep healthy and in shape.

In case you haven't read my book *I Am Not A Victim, I Am A Survivor,* the reason why the gym triggers a lot of trauma responses within me is because of the sportswear. I was raped in sportswear so seeing it all and having to see hot guys in sportswear is very hard for me.

It reminds me too much of my rape.

Therefore, a lot of me and my counsellor discussed is the same as the DnD content in terms of remembering and holding onto that physical feeling of safety. As well as take small steps so over time I can spend more and more time in the gym.

In addition, she did mention how I could desensitise myself to the sensory experiences of a gym too. For example, the smell, the sounds and more that's associated with the gym. Even if it's someone taking their belt off because that was an extremely distressing noise for me that me and my best friend found out the hard way. I had no idea that was such a triggering sound until it was far too late one night.

As a result, my idea was that I would sit in the gym café when there are all the gym people in their sportswear walking around, and I would do some work on my laptop. This would allow me to become desensitised to sportswear as it shows I can be around sportswear without anything bad happening to me.

Then I could build up going into the gym and working out.

Fast-forward six weeks later, I have only sat in the gym café once but that was at least a month after this session and by that time, my

PTSD and other trauma reactions were dramatically reduced so it was fine. As well as I think I could easily go to the gym now and work out with my friends but given my eating disorder, I don't want to risk it.

As much as I have anorexic thinking, I am trying not to dramatically lose too many calories.

<u>Social Groups</u>

Finally, the Thursday before this counselling session, I went out with a new friend that I had made, let's call them Joe and their boyfriend. Originally, me and my housemates were meant to be going out with them for dinner but they all had to go back. Ruby was struggling so my best friend went to support them and my other housemate had a society event on then they went home afterwards as me, Joe and their boyfriend were talking.

Joe's boyfriend was an overweight man with long brown hair, exactly like my rapist. It was difficult for me for sure so I focused on Joe and the three of us chatted for two or three hours.

However, around nine o'clock in the evening, I started seriously dipping and I knew I needed to go. I forgot to mention that in my previous counselling session she had spoken to me about how I need to just go whenever I'm feeling down.

The issue on this particular night was that I had already offered them lifts home and I had never asked someone to just leave before. So I hung it out for another 15 minutes until I texted Joe (yes, the person sitting straight across from me) about me dipping and can we go.

If I had just left them that night then I might have been okay, but I didn't. We all walked back to my car and I drove them home. The walk to my car (on the other side of campus) was the longest part but I kept dipping more and more.

When I eventually got home, I had a mental health crisis, I couldn't stop shaking, my PTSD was kicked into high gear and it was a rough night. It was something about being stuck with two people in the enclosed space of my car that really bothered me. In my mind, Joe and their boyfriend could have done whatever they wanted to me and I wouldn't have been able to stop it.

That is what caused my crisis.

Anyway, I explained this to my counsellor and she was very empathetic and compassionate, because that was the first time I had ever practised the skill. As well as it's great that I did want to leave at some point, I didn't make it last any longer than needed.

Overall, in the future, I needed to do the same remembering and focusing on the physical feeling of safety as previously mentioned. Also, I needed to remember that if I am dipping then I NEED to go immediately. Then over time as my trauma responses get better and better, I can work myself towards being able to take people home.

Thankfully, 6 weeks on I have done that very well. I have driven new ambassadors at my university to and from work opportunities without a breakdown and everything is really good.

In a few chapters' time, you get to see how I met up with someone one-on-one for the first time since my rape.

Finally, I made my counsellor cry because I have had such a powerfully healing moment this week that I was able to change something in my perspective towards December. You see my best friend is going to Thailand to see some new family members for the first time so they won't be here for 10 days then they'll be staying with their family in the Midlands afterwards.

Therefore, we both found that us calling every day worked really well in August 2024. I was so depressed, suicidal and I was not able to do much of anything. At the start of the collapse of my mental health, it took me 5 hours just to have a shower.

We were going to call every day again when they were in Thailand and back in the Midlands for mental health support. Yet this particular week, I was able to say to my best friend "I don't want to call because you're my mental health support or you're my carer, I want to call every day because you're my best friend,"

I was only able to say that and make my counsellor cry because I had had a healing moment. You can have your healing moment too with the right support, counselling and friends.

WHAT IS THE THREE STAGE TRAUMA RECOVERY MODEL?

As a psychology Masters student at the time of writing with a massive interest in clinical psychology, I really like looking into therapies. This is even more true when I'm undergoing therapy and counselling for trauma, so when I found out my rape counselling was based on the Three-Stage Recovery Model by Judith Herman, I wanted to learn more. Granted, it took me 9 weeks to finally get round to researching the model in-depth but better late than never. Therefore, in this chapter, you'll learn what are the three stages included in this recovery model, why are they useful and how does the model work to treat trauma. If you enjoy learning about mental health, clinical trauma work and psychotherapy then this is a brilliant chapter for you.

What Is The Three-Stage Recovery Model By Judith Herman?

The more I read about trauma work and the psychological models designed to explain how to treat trauma, the more I realise how important American psychiatrist Judith Herman's recovery model actually is. This model forms the foundation of a lot of psychotherapies as well as it is the basis of the specialist rape counselling that I underwent between September and December 2024. I technically have one session left at the time of writing but we've done all the therapeutic work.

Personally, whilst I'll explain this model in a moment, as a psychology student, podcaster and writer, I find this model immensely useful. Since it explains how to deal with the trauma responses and gradually helps a client to return to a clinically normal life where they can control their actions, do the activities they want to do and they can enjoy life again.

As a client with sexual trauma, I found this model even more useful. It isn't a linear model which bugged me and my autistic brain, but it is very helpful. It allowed me to basically get rid of my Post-Traumatic Stress Disorder, decrease my triggers dramatically and I can actually do things again with my life. For example, last week, I went out with a new friend one-on-one for the first time since my rape. That was amazing and so major for me because before the very notion of spending one-on-one time with anyone but my best friend would cause me to have a mental health crisis.

Ultimately, the three stages of the recovery model are:

- Safety and Stabilisation
- Remembrance and Mourning
- Reconnection and Integration

During each of these stages, the therapist works with the client to create an environment where the client can safely process what happened to them without any sense of urgency. This helps to ensure the recovery is sustainable as well as empowering.

What Is the Safety and Stabilisation Stage?

The first stage of the recovery model is the "Safety and Stabilisation" stage and when I've looked into trauma work in a psychotherapy context I've always heard rumours about stabilisation work, but it is only through my counselling that I was able to see what that looks like. Therefore, stabilisation work is the very bedrock and foundation of all the therapy work that happens afterwards. The client absolutely needs to feel physically and emotionally safe before they can ever hope to engage with their trauma.

There is a real-world caveat here but I'll address it later.

In addition, a large focus for the therapist during stabilisation work is to build a rapport and ensure that clients feel comfortable with them. I always say how as therapists we are asking clients to reveal their own personal, dark moments to us, people who are effectively strangers. That takes a lot of courage and a lot of trust, so we need to earn that trust quickly and effectively.

One technique of helping clients feel comfortable is that trauma-informed counsellors must be prepared to disclose small amounts of personal information about themselves if the client asks a question. This is useful in building trust. Especially, as there is a relationship between the client and therapist called the therapeutic alliance, and if I adopt a marketing term "we buy from people we know, like and trust". We can adapt this idea to psychology because "we like working with therapists, we know, like and trust". Therefore, having a therapist open up to us about themselves helps us to know them so we can hopefully like them and trust them after a while too.

Judith Herman herself uses the comparison that clients like to know who's "holding the rope" during their therapy sessions so they can develop their sense of safety. Just like how a climber likes to know who's holding their rope (safety line) during a climbing challenge.

Moreover, stabilisation work involves reducing chaos and crisis in a client's life so this might involve helping them to create a sense or environment of normalcy within the therapeutic environment. This helps the client to feel secure enough to explore their trauma. Especially, because trauma survivors typically feel unsafe internally (within themselves) as well as externally (in the physical world). This is why trauma-informed therapists work with clients to understand the difference between their internal and external realities and help them to learn techniques to manage hyperarousal and other trauma responses.

In another chapter, you'll learn about Window of Tolerance for this reason.

On the whole, stabilisation work focuses on stabilisation techniques like psychoeducation, self-regulation and boundary-setting strategies. As well as therapists don't force disclosures or force progress too quickly because clients need to be able to progress their trauma at their own speed. Also, therapists help clients during stabilisation work to reduce chaos and crisis in their life, create a safe space and give the clients tools to help them separate their internal and external realities. Something that is highly useful for dealing with flashbacks and other trauma responses.

<u>What Is The Remembrance and Mourning Stage?</u>

The second stage of Herman's recovery model is the Remembrance and Mourning stage that focuses on reconstructing the trauma through remembrance and then mourning. Unfortunately, clients can experience this stage as a timeless descent with no clear endpoint.

Interestingly enough, I actually experienced this sense and it was painful because it felt like I was processing things, remembering a lot of awful details about my rape but I didn't know what I was working towards. I didn't even know where the counselling was heading towards and I felt confused that I wasn't expressively telling her what happened during my rape.

Additionally, during this second stage, it isn't unusual for clients to experience grief over various losses in their lives. For example, their loss of innocence, some failed relationships and even loss of family support or friends. This is important to remember when we consider that a lot of survivors, even more so for survivors abused within families, are often rejected or are faced with disbelief when they disclose their trauma. This leads clients to feel isolated as trauma can sever family ties.

This connects to the topic of Rape Grief that I talk about in *I Am A Survivor, Not A Victim.*

Moving onto the mourning aspect of this stage, I was no exception to this issue, a lot of clients mourn over the loss of years (or months) that their trauma has controlled their life. Clients feel like the trauma has robbed them of time that could have been spent in healthy relationships, personal growth and fulfilling careers. This is why it's important that therapists support clients with empathy and without judgment so the client isn't rushed.

Personally, when it came to my childhood trauma, I was angry for so long that I wasn't able to form healthy friendships, relationships, get a boyfriend, kiss and enjoy so many normal things that normal teenagers are allowed to do. I mourned that loss for so, so long. Equally, when it came to my sexual trauma, I mourned for months that I was going through my PTSD, intense social anxiety, depression and all my other trauma responses. I mourned for the lost friendships, the lost ability to do fun things and I mourned for the impact it had/ has (still present tenses to be fair) on my writing, podcasting and everything else that I flat out love.

During this second stage, the therapist's main job is to help a client process these losses and provide a safe space for a client to recount their trauma without the pressure of time or any expectations. Clarity, courage and trust are all needed for therapists and clients throughout this stage.

What is The Reconnection and Integration Stage of The Recovery Model?

In the final stage of the model, therapists work with clients to help them work towards reconnecting with their world as well as integrating their trauma into a new sense of self. For example, during this stage, clients regain trust in their relationships because they've learnt how to extend their trust and when it's best not to extend trust to someone. As well as this stage involves something called "reparenting". I first came across this term in my counselling during August 2023 and this is a term that describes the therapist's role in modelling healthy boundaries as well as relationships. When it comes to trauma survivors, this can include relearning what are, how to have and how to recognise healthy sexual relationships. Something that myself and a lot of different survivors find immensely difficult, because this "reparenting" is often the first time that someone has spoken to us about what on Earth healthy relationships look like.

In addition, a major part of reconnection during this stage is the survivor developing and maintaining their ability to form and sustain healthy relationships. This doesn't only mean sexual relationships, but it can include friendships and familial relationships too. I talk a lot about these aspects of my trauma recovery in my book *Healing As A Survivor*. Also, for survivors of sexual abuse and sexual violence, a lot of survivors have to rediscover their sexual identity and sexual preferences, which is immensely challenging, because this only adds to the struggle that survivors have around their sense of self.

Furthermore, you tend to be able to see progress in this stage of trauma recovery in a few different ways. For instance, as clients progress, they can enjoy intimacy or new experiences without associating it with their abuser or feeling like they need to be protected from their abuser. And the reason why these are amazing, wonderful moments for survivors is because they show the client is growing in their autonomy and ability to live without the fear and trauma responses that have ruled their life for so long.

I know for me, being able to go out with a newish friend one-on-one was an amazing experience, because for the past 7 months that would have been flat out impossible. It would have caused me to have a panic attack, a breakdown and I would have had constant trauma responses. That had happened a good few times.

However, this is a difficult and scary stage of trauma recovery because it's an immensely weird and disorienting feeling to know that you don't need to be protected from your attacker. Also, it is so disorienting to feel safe, secure and able to experience life and pleasure without trauma responses. I talk more about this in my healing book, but I found it weird because I had been having severe PTSD for 7 months and then I wasn't.

It was weird to experience such an extreme change.

Conclusion

As much as I love the trauma recovery model because I have experienced it in the real world and I know how it can transform lives for the better, it isn't the best applied psychological model. Since the model itself proposes that these stages are very linear, but in reality, you tend to work through all these stages at the same time to different extents. When I was talking to my counsellor about this model, she explained how we work a lot on Stage 1 at the beginning but during stabilization work, you are processing the trauma too, and doing a little integration work too. Whereas towards the end of the therapy, you're working more on integration work and less on processing trauma and stabilisation work, but those stages are still present too.

Ultimately, the Three-Stage Recovery Model is a humane and thorough model that provides a helpful framework for trauma therapy. It focuses on client safety and respecting client autonomy during the healing process because the model stresses it is the client that controls their pace, not the therapist. Then the therapist facilitates the client's recovery by respecting the complex nature of trauma and provides the client with a safe space. As well as therapists and clients need to understand what can be achieved in the limited number of sessions that a mental health service provides so it's easier to maintain realistic therapeutic goals.

Yet we need to remember as aspiring and qualified psychologists that trauma work is not easy on *us*.

I know I always talk about how important focusing on our clients are but honestly, we are so important too. We cannot help people if we don't look after ourselves and if our mental health isn't as good as it could be. Therefore, clinical supervision and self-care are critical for therapists because trauma work takes an emotional toll on us so we need to practice good self-care and we need to balance what our clients need with our capacity. As well as trauma-informed therapists should receive ongoing professional support so regular discussions in supervision and peer consultations can be useful in maintaining their effectiveness and well-being. Finally, a supportive work environment is important too so therapists and clients can work in a safe environment and have the time needed for meaningful, sustained healing.

That will ultimately change our client's life for the better.

INTENSE TWO WEEKS, HEARTBREAK AT HOME AND PTSD IS NOT FUN: LESSONS FROM A SEVENTH SESSION

Note: you absolutely have to read the "Self-Compassion Steps" section in this chapter. It was a major healing technique for me, so it should help you too.

As a fellow survivor, person who works with survivors or you have a survivor in your life then you might be extremely well aware at this point that everything in healing depends on context. Therefore, for context, there was a two-week gap between my last session and this one because my counsellor needed to go away for a week to deal with a family matter.

Originally, I thought these two weeks were going to be great, really easy and great for my mental health because I felt safe, I felt secure and my PTSD was really starting to decrease. Whilst that was completely true in the second week, the first week did not want to follow my hopes and dreams.

My mental health died yet again for another few reasons that I will mention in this chapter, because they're insightful, they're helpful for understanding sexual trauma and its impact and there is a certain comedy in one of these events looking back.

Learning About A Massive Change In My Personal Life

I fully admit that looking back this was almost funny that I reacted this way to this specific event, but at the time, this was one of the most intense, awful and shocking 48 hours of my life. A lot happened and it was awful.

On the Sunday night of the first week, me and my housemates were hanging out in my best friend's bedroom talking, catching up and just spending time together. I was already feeling really low and my mental health wasn't great because sexual trauma is horrible. As well as me and my best friend had scheduled to spend some time together just the two of us and it was nine o'clock at night and it hadn't happened yet. I later found out we needed to plan something specific so it would happen and thankfully we've done a lot of great things since.

Yet at the time one of my very old friends from school had contacted me so I was writing out a message to her (after talking to her for the first time in years, no one can accuse me of writing too long messages again).

However, as I was writing this message, I started hearing kissing sounds that two people were making out. Bearing in mind I have never been kissed, no one has even made out with me and my rapist was the first person to ever kiss me.

My PTSD kicked in and I ran out the room after shouting out "No!".

Afterwards my best friend came to check on me and we went out into their room to spend some time together just the two of us and talk about it and then my best friend just dropped a bombshell.

Now bear in mind, that I love my best friend romantically. They are the kindest person you will ever meet, and they are sweet, thoughtful and they are attractive too, but it's *them* and their personality that I love.

I asked them back in October 2023, they said no but they wanted to become good friends with me anyway.

My best friend told me that they were dating Ruby, our other housemate, and I felt so bad, so awful and it felt like my world was collapsing down around me.

I think I felt this way because I am so used to my best friend's partners being online, living hundreds of miles away or them dating dickheads. And most importantly, I never had to see their partners and see another person kiss, hug and sleep with the person I wanted to.

Yes, I am only human after all.

Yet we kept talking, spending time together and I was relatively okay when they went to bed with Ruby, but the problem was that my mind spiralled with distress. It brought up all my child abuse, all my sexual trauma and all my crippling grief about never being able to find love, be in a relationship and find someone who would love me without raping me.

My mind kept running a million times an hour so I wanted to self-soothe. The breathing wasn't working, I was too distressed to listen to music or read so I went for a walk.

I know going for a walk is a good way to calm down.

Everything got even worse.

As summarised in this message I wrote out in an effort to talk to a helpline:

"What happened tonight was I was already feeling depressed and distressed because I found out my best friend and another friend of ours are dating. And it's naturally hard because I romantically love my best friend and we're both open and accepting about that fact and that Blue will never love me romantically but they love me as a friend.

And I realised a PTSD trigger for me is hearing constant kissing. One or two kisses is fine so that's why no one knew, including me, thought it was a trigger before.

Then I went to bed, I couldn't self-sooth so I went for a walk. I got triggered and went into full survival mode with panic attacks and everything because I remembered like tonight, I was raped on a cold night, all the houses in the dark looks like my rapist's house and I went for a walk around the time I was raped. Then there were other people about who I perceived as dangerous and so on.

I came back to the house my best friend comforted me for 25 mins. They didn't want to go but they were really tired and they encouraged me to use a helpline if needed.

I'm too exhausted and scared and nervous about a helpline to use it.

That was all 2 hours ago and I'm still distressed."

Interestingly, my best friend kept saying to me to try a helpline but I didn't know how to use one so I contacted one via the online chat, it went through but I instantly logged back off it because I didn't know how it worked.

I simply kept panicking, getting more and more distressed and I felt like I was going to die because the little bombshell of my two friends dating had brought up so much trauma for me.

The Next Day: Even Worse Bad News

After three hours sleep, I woke up still very distressed, constantly shaking and I went downstairs to make myself some breakfast. I panicked so much when I was downstairs I collapsed to the ground then I went upstairs to get ready for a shower but my thoughts were still going so fast and my heart felt like it was going to explode so I collapsed again and I couldn't get back up.

I was meant to take my best friend to therapy that morning but I was collapsed on the floor in my doorway so they helped me back into bed and took the bus to therapy.

I felt awful. I felt like such a failure as a friend, an idiot and I hated that I was reacting so badly to the fact that they were in a relationship with such a lovely person.

I fell off my bed whilst they were out and when they texted me saying they were almost back I tried to go down the stairs but I collapsed going down them. Thankfully, I managed to grab the stair rail so I wasn't injured too badly.

Then me and my best friend spoke and they broke my heart yet again.

They told me they couldn't support me as much anymore.

The one singular constant in my life, the one person who was the only person I could turn to and the one person I trusted to let touch me was stepping away from me.

My heart shattered.

Why did they say this I hear you ask.

As a result of their mental health was starting to decline now and they flat out hated seeing me so distressed, me trying to kill myself and they kept having panic attacks over the thought of me dying. They said how they were

terrified that I was going to die because of their inaction.

And they were only just realising that they weren't entirely comfortable with us cuddling so that was starting to impact them too. That was something that has always bugged me about my best friend, because one of the ways their autism manifests is that they don't realise something is bothering them until it's become part of our friendship.

They've done this before and it always hurts me, but I know they genuinely don't mean to do this on purpose. As well as, as soon as they find out something is hurting them, they do find a solution so our friendship is okay.

I still get hurt in the end anyway.

Nonetheless, it would be easy for me to protest and say that anyone who hurts me isn't worth being in my life. Then in the next chapter, we're going to be talking about the Traffic Light system and I explain there how people can do Yellow Lights without meaning and as long as they learn from their mistakes and try then it is okay in the end.

And friends hurting you by accident isn't ideal, but that is part of friendship and interacting with other humans.

If we lose ourselves off and cut off everyone who makes a mistake and hurts us, then all our lives would be extremely lonely and boring indeed.

Nonetheless, in this moment, I was extremely hurt and I was in so much emotional pain because honestly… I was annoyed at my best friend. I was the one that kept asking for permission and consent, I was the one holding back for asking what I needed because I wanted my best friend to be okay.

They went to Yellow boundaries with me to make sure I was okay. I was grateful for it in the moment but looking back this was one of the massive mistakes they made with our friendship.

<u>Online Rape Crisis Chats</u>

As a result of my best friend taking a major step back, they wanted me to start using helplines so I found one and they sat with me whilst I used it. I still had no idea how to use a helpline so I wrote out the following message and it helps to capture a lot of my raw emotion on the day:

"I got extremely triggered last night that my best friend (who I have unrequited love for) and my housemate were making out (I didn't know they were a couple before that). None of us knew kissing was trigger for me before because it's happened before but not making out. So I had severe PTSD reactions to the kissing.

Then after this PTSD episode my best friend told me they're dating.

I feel silly but that made me worse because I want both of them to be happy but it's dating in the house when I already struggle with feelings that I'll never be loved, able to date or anything and this changes everything in the house and my relationship with them.

They're both confirmed to be everything is fine, nothing is going to change (and honestly it actually won't) but it's hard.

Then I went for a walk. Before remembering something I had repressed. I was raped on a cold night and I walked some of the way there in the cold. And a lot of the houses where I recently moved look like my rapist's house in the dark.

I have been having panic attacks for 18

hours with only 3 hours not because I was sleeping. I'm exhausted, and struggling."

As you can see, I was really distressed and I was not hopeful about the effectiveness of online chats. I really wasn't hopeful because I had no idea how using an online chat and texting a random stranger would be useful.

Turns out it was useful.

I used the Rape Crisis England and Wales online chat and you're allowed to use it twice a week for 45 minutes. By the end of the 45 minutes, I was much more relaxed and I wasn't panicking quite as much and I felt relatively okay.

Since that night, I have probably used the online chat four times. I've had one bad experience because there was a worker who clearly didn't understand that men could be raped too, I've had two good experiences and I a flat out amazing experience.

Therefore, if you are struggling, definitely contact a helpline because these people are trained to listen to and believe you and signpost you to mental health and other services.

I cannot recommend them enough.

Finally, for this section, the next day I was actually bed-bound because I was so malnourished I felt like I was going to die. I think it was a mixture of malnourishment from my eating disorder, the extreme stress of Sunday night and Monday and me not sleeping enough.

PTSD Is Not Fun: A Birthday Celebration and a London Bus

The rest of these sections should be shorter as I highlight specific situations. For example, a week before my seventh therapy session, it was my best friend's birthday celebration so they had their nine friends around to watch the first Lord of the Rings film extended edition.

There were a lot of people, I was still adjusting to my new reality of needing to make decisions myself and me supporting myself more. I used the online chat again to calm myself down and I used some self-care techniques and other self-soothing ideas to get myself ready for the birthday party.

I was calm but it did not last long.

When you get a group of young people together, there were bound to be sexual comments made and my PTSD at this point in time does not respond well to sexual references.

I was already severely distressed so it only took one comment and I ran out the room as fast as I could.

My best friend came to check on me and I just couldn't deal with their birthday anymore, and I certainly couldn't make a decision about what to order for dinner. That alone caused me to have a panic attack, so me, Ruby and my best friend shared a massive pizza together.

The advantages of me and Ruby both having eating disorders. We can support each other in tiny ways.

What was meant to be a birthday celebration turned into a nightmare for me, my trauma and my PTSD.

Then the day before my seventh counselling session, we went up to London together and whilst my best friend spoke on a London bus, I heard a woman reporting sexual harassment and sure, my PTSD kicked in. Yet it wasn't as intense as before as much as my mind tried to tell me I was in danger, I was going to die and I was going to get raped again.

My PTSD had decreased and that was a weird feeling in its own right.

<u>Self-Compassionate Steps</u>

This was a critical part of my own healing journey because I have never been very self-compassionate but once you realise it is okay to show compassion with yourself. Your life will change forever in a very, very good way and it takes a little bit of time to practise but it is a great technique to use.

Therefore, Doctor Kristin Neff developed the following five steps to help you become self-compassionate:

1. Understand shame is normal and it doesn't need to be eliminated. It is okay to feel shame.
2. Acknowledge you are hurting and you are distressed.
3. Understand other people go through the same thing.
4. Pretend you're talking to a dear friend that is going through the same thing as you. What would you say to them?
5. Say that to yourself and take it in. Internalise what you would say to a dear friend.

Be your friend for a change. Treat yourself as you would a friend, never treat yourself as an enemy.

So to use these self-compassionate steps with the PTSD example at the birthday celebration, I would:

1. Acknowledge that I was distressed about being in a large group, having to support myself as much as I could and I was hurting that my best friend was in a relationship with someone who wasn't me.
2. It's okay to feel like this because other people hurt when people who they are interested in are no longer available, and lots of other survivors experience anxiety.
3. I would ensure my dear friend that it's okay to feel like this. It doesn't make them a bad person, a bad friend and it doesn't make them weak. It just means they are a survivor of something awful and they are healing. They can come down whenever they want, they can choose to say upstairs and they do whatever they need to do. Because they are important too.
4. And I would say that to myself and accept it, because it is all true.

Self-compassion often requires practice but it is so important.

<u>Quick Note On Session Itself and A Transactional Analysis Technique</u>

After all the chaos of the past two weeks, it was a really good session that was positive, we were both really pleased with my progress and how much I was healing and everything I had discovered about myself.

We did some extra paperwork using the centre's CORE outcome measurements which was a questionnaire about the severity of my symptoms, ability to function and more.

Moreover, I learnt about something called "Okay Corral". It's an idea that comes from an approach to therapy called Transactional Analysis (TA). I don't like a lot of what TA does because it's psychodynamic but there are some good concepts.

"Okay Corral" is about there are four types of interpersonal situations:

- Me and the other person are okay.
- I am okay but the other person is not.
- I am not okay but the other person is.
- We are both not okay.

My counsellor mentioned this to me because she thought this technique might be useful to remember if I'm feeling tense, awful or nervous in a social situation. I can think about which category this situation falls into and what I need to do to be okay.

Using the order listed above, I might do the following:

- Not change anything because we are both okay.
- I would try to help the other person but I would prepare to leave.
- I would use my self-soothing and other therapy techniques. If they didn't work then I would leave the situation. I might consider asking for social support but that depends on the other person.
- We should both leave because no one is okay.

Overall, I think this is a useful tool if you're struggling in a social situation and your trauma starts making you feel unsafe or like the other person hates you. That is a train of thought my brain loves to tell me, but that's not entirely related to sexual trauma.

Remember it for the future.

Finally, we agreed that in the next session, we're going to look at interpersonal red flags so I can recognise abuse and manipulation in the future.

A very important and critical life skill for everyone. Especially, survivors and I hope you learn as much as I did in the next chapter.

Turn over the page and let's find out.

SELF-COMPASSION, ADJUSTING TO A NEW REALITY AND LEARNING TO RECOGNISE ABUSE: LESSONS LEARNT FROM SESSION EIGHT

This next week proved that I was partly struggling to adapt to the new reality of me and my best friend wanting a healthier relationship where they supported me less, but I was still able to talk to, text and call them if needed.

The theme of the week was certainly me taking their boundary too far (I may have accidentally cut myself off completely from them in terms of support) with sprinkles of self-compassion and recognising abuse in the process too.

Therefore, I wanted to share this chapter with you because I want you to realise that it is okay if you take actions a little too far after someone imposes a boundary. It is okay if you misinterpret things and it is okay if you get distressed and "overreact" to what a dear friend has said.

Whilst you are healing, you are going through hell and back and you are trying to survive as best you can. The world already seems like a dangerous place, the world is confusing and every single thing you thought you knew about the world gets turned on its head after sexual violence.

It is normal to react in ways that other people think are overreacting.

You are surviving and that is why you are so amazing, because you are able to survive. Now the next stage of healing is to calm your body down and retrain your brain so it doesn't need to go on survival mode so often when it doesn't need to.

Proved I Can Do Self-Compassion and Triggers Majorly Decreasing

After my best friend told me they need to take a step back last week, we spoke about how I need more friends that over time I could deepen those relationships and I could have additional people to turn to for support.

I had no idea how to do this because friendships were always messy, complicated and everyone always seemed to leave me in the end anyway. Between childhood trauma and autism, making friendships always feels like an impossible task, but thankfully my best friend understood to.

Everyone in my shared university house is autistic.

However, one option we did come up with was that my university has a Warhammer 40,000 society (just think a social group formed around a particular interest for our international audience). As a teenager, I had loved Warhammer 40,000 because it's a great science fiction fantasy game and even now I listen to a Warhammer podcast, watch lore videos and I still keep a pulse on the hobby.

As a result, my best friend managed to begrudgingly convince me to go on Saturday, so my parents thankfully paid for me to get some models (they are stupidly expensive. Another great reason why I stopped playing Warhammer. My bank account didn't like it), so I tried to go.

Now I hadn't realised until I tried to go to Warhammer society that Saturday that this was the first time I had tried to go to a brand-new event alone since my rape.

I had always gone to events or work opportunities that I was familiar with pre-rape. I could easily manage those events or situations because they weren't new and I was familiar with them before my rape, but this was a brand-new situation. I didn't have any friends with me, I didn't have any support and so my PTSD kicked in.

I hid in a university toilet for a few hours constantly cycling between pure fear, anxiety and panic attacks. Then I tried more and more to get up the courage to get going again and I couldn't.

I was trapped in a cycle of fear, panic and rape memories so I never ended up going.

I spent around three hours at the university before my best friend was done with their Dungeons and Dragons game, so we went back to our place together.

We spoke about how terrified I was that I was going to get raped again by going to the Warhammer society alone. And they reminded me that's it's okay that it takes time to build up the courage and confidence to do new things, and after it became clear I wasn't able to go *today*, I should have left and gone home to self-soothe.

That was a great note for future reference.

Over to you dear reader, I want you to know that it's okay if you can't do things straight away. I mention all the distressing times when I tried to do basic or social things I simply couldn't in my book *I Am Not A Victim, I Am A Survivor*. Yet I want you to be aware that you will fall into the trap at some point of "oh I've healed a little that means I am cured and I can do everything,". Whilst it is definitely true you will be able to do so much more as you heal, there will be limits as you edge towards the tail end of your healing journey.

For example, at this point of my healing journey, I could be in the same room and talk to a fat man, I could hear sexual references and see implied sexual scenes in films amongst other things. Yet at this point, I couldn't do something brand-new by myself.

Like a lot of these chapters, I'm writing them a good few weeks after the session happened based on my notes, but now I am able to go out to brand-new things. Such as, I just came back from a brand-new "Winter Showcase" at my university where PhD students were presenting their research. I saw two presentations on "carbonwashing" and "how Working From Home impacts Fertility rates". Both of them were very good presentations and I was talking to a guy I found attractive in the break before I went home.

It was a good few hours out, I got to talk to a few really nice people and it was something I wouldn't have been able to do a few weeks ago. I am only able to do it now because I am healed enough to do new things.

Around the time of my seventh session, I wasn't healed enough but now I am. Therefore, please know that things do get better if you keep slowly working towards healing, be kind to yourself and keep trying in the future.

Finally, for this section, a major sign that my triggers are decreasing was when Chloe (a fake name) came round the Thursday before this session for some video games and a catch-up. I walked them back. It was a cold, dark night through where I live, exactly the same as the night I had been extremely triggered and had panic attacks for 18 hours.

I was fine, because I was just that little bit more healed and I had spent a lovely evening with my housemates and Chloe.

<u>Adjusting To A New Reality</u>

Since my best friend took a massive step back in terms of supporting me, my brain was struggling to cope with this new reality so it made me take their boundary too far and I cut myself off from their support. This wasn't great for my mental health as you can imagine because it left me feeling very isolated, lonely and like I had no one I could turn to when I needed it.

I was still using the rape crisis online chat, self-soothing techniques and other tools I had at my disposal, but it was hard for me. It was hard for me to adapt to a massive change in our relationship.

As a result, on the Sunday before this session happened, we both spoke about it during our scheduled time together (no autistic signs there, ha.) and my best friend was worried that I had cut them off and I was distressed that I was completely alone. Especially, as since they had started dating Ruby, they weren't talking to me about emotional stuff so I felt less close to them and like our friendship was nothing compared to what it had been.

The conclusion of our conversation was that my best friend needed to talk to me more so I could get what I needed from the relationship, and my best friend wanted me to lean on them more. It was all about trying to find a middle ground as we explored what a healthy relationship looked like.

Now this connects to the counselling session because she helped me to realise (and one of the women on the rape online chat had helped me with the same thing) that it's okay that my best friend hurt me, that we both made mistakes and it was bad that they didn't tell me when they weren't comfortable with something we were doing or consider the consequences of what we were doing, like cuddling for support.

Then towards the end of this segment of the session, my counsellor mentioned if we've spoken about what a healthy relationship looks like for both of us. Thankfully, we had the Sunday before this session.

For us, a healthy relationship evolves over time and it is where we support each other. We can always text, talk to and call the other for support, but there are boundaries. We still hug because that's what my best friend likes doing with their friends, but we don't cuddle, I don't stay in their room anymore and then I added that we focus on our actual friendship.

We focus less on support for mental health, and more on why we're actually friends and that takes centre stage of "us" instead of my best friend effectively being a carer. We focus on all our shared interests, our shared points of view and we do things together because we like hanging out. Not because I need the support.

I won't lie, this was and still is a tough reality to get used to, but over time I have gotten better and our relationship is lovely. It can still be distressing when I want support but I know I need to do a lot more for myself these days and that's okay.

They are still my best friend, they are still there for me and we are still great together. Which is brilliant news considering we recently extended the tenancy agreement for another year.

How To Recognise Manipulation

We spent about the final twenty minutes of the session discussing how to recognise manipulation and abuse. In the next two chapters, I'll include content on coercive control and gaslighting because it goes into more depth than I can in this chapter.

Understanding gaslighting and control is very important for survivors.

In the session itself, there was a lot of to-and-fro because I didn't understand signs of abuse. No one ever taught it to me in school because you never get taught about what healthy relationships look like and you never get taught about abuse. That is a massive failure of the education system, similar to what I talk about in *Breaking The Silence* with teenage dating violence.

As a result, abuse and manipulation is a pattern that can be very sophisticated. It isn't often mean things that typically align with the "traditional" view of abuse and manipulation. In reality, abuse are often nice things that the abuser uses to isolate you from your social support system.

For example, in my case, it would be my abuser would be trying to separate me and prevent me from spending time with my best friend and other housemates. He might "treat" me to a nice dinner, maybe surprise cinema tickets and so on.

Anything that he can disguise as a so-called nice treat to continue to isolate me away from my support system until I become dependent on him. That is how abuse and manipulation typically works in the real world.

My counsellor went to say that when I notice this pattern, I need to have a conversation to correct it and remember to balance my time between myself, my partner and my social support network.

This connects to skills you learn about in specialist counselling about saying no and setting boundaries. I would need to say no to my abuser because if I had plans to spend time with my housemates that night and my abuser would surprise me by taking me away from them. I should say no to him and continue my plans with my housemates.

And resist any emotional manipulation he tries.

Please note, I'm using *he* because I'm attracted to mainly men and transmasculine individuals but women and transfeminine people could do this just as easily.

Therefore, it's important to have a conversation to correct this behaviour and set up boundaries. In the current example, I could set a boundary saying my partner needs to stop surprising me, needs to respect the time I spend with other people and I need more room for myself.

In reality, I might only set one of those boundaries for starters, because it's okay to be nervous about setting new boundaries. Especially after what you, the reader, and me have been through.

Yet boundaries are so important to set and reinforce like I mentioned in previous chapters.

If the partner doesn't respect your boundaries and this person continues to manipulate you and isolate you from your social support system. Then you need to leave and end the relationship as hard as it seems, and thankfully there are a lot of great resources available online for you if needed.

The final activity my counsellor wanted us to discuss was considering what makes actions and partners go from "Green Light" (meaning everything is okay) to "Yellow Light" (meaning you're uncomfortable and you might withdraw consent but it isn't an automatic No) to a "Red Light". This means the other person has crossed a line and you want to withdraw consent immediately.

This was a hard activity because I had never thought what actions or what could make someone go through these different boundaries.

I highly recommend that you think about this yourself. Both in terms of sexual consent and what partners are allowed to do in everyday life.

Personally, an action is Green Light if I am okay with it and it doesn't make me uncomfortable at all. My Healing Sexual Trauma Workbook made me write about what this feels like in terms of my body and I wrote "when it's a *yes* boundary, I feel happy, relaxed and excited." These activities depend on the person but these can include kissing, hugging and cuddling.

In addition, for me a Yellow Light is something I am not entirely comfortable with and I need to think about it. It is perfectly okay to stop during sex, think about it in another room and then continue.

Your safety is the most important thing.

If a partner makes me uncomfortable then I will talk to them and set a boundary on it so we might not do it at all or we can do it in a way that makes me feel safe and respected.

This can apply to the relationship itself too, because if my partner accidentally tells a secret to someone I know, that doesn't make them a bad person. People are not perfect in relationships and both of you will make mistakes, and it doesn't make you a bad person if you learn from them.

Therefore, if my partner made a mistake that made me feel uncomfortable then I would talk to them so they wouldn't do it again.

Finally, in terms of Red lights, for sexual relationships, this would be anything I am not comfortable with and any sexual acts that make me feel scared, nervous and make me start or want to start shaking. In terms of romantic relationships, this is whenever someone crosses a boundary that they are aware of and they don't listen or respect me when I reinforce it.

People who go into Red Lights and don't learn from their mistakes do not deserve to be in your life.

It is as simple as that because you are the most important person in your life and your safety is beyond vital.

Never forget that dear reader.

WHAT IS COERCIVE CONTROL?

After learning about recognising buse and manipulation in relationships, and coming across a woman's domestic violence survival story and her wish to raise awareness about domestic violence and Coercive Control. I really wanted to help honour her survival in a way so I wanted us to look on the podcast at this critical topic. So we can understand the psychology behind this outrageous behaviour, and in future episodes hopefully focus on helping ourselves avoid Coercive control.

Why Psychology Needs To Look At Coercive Control And Abusive Relationships?

I always think it's important to highlight why these are important topics to discuss on the podcast because that way I know I tend to focus on them, and you might enjoy them more because of their importance. I don't know why I like to lay down a psychological foundation too before we dive into the meat of the topic.

In terms of Coercive Control and abusive relationships, many people simply ask questions: *why don't victims simply leave the relationship?*

And of course that is a reasonable question, I think when I was younger I wondered that too. Yet from social psychology and the Need To Belong Theory, humans are resistant to breaking any relationship even ones that are bad for us.

In addition, as we are all hopefully outside the abusive relationship the answer seems so simple to the abuse. Just report it and leave the relationship. But this is where the reality is different from the ideal and it was a lot, lot more complicated than this.

As well as whilst there are many different reasons why victims don't leave the relationship. One of the most common reasons is fear, and whilst the exact definition of fear is hard to pin down. A good definition is something along the lines of a very unpleasant strong emotion caused by a person's anticipation and/ or awareness of danger.

Due to like most emotions, fear can range from minor to severe, and the fear could be real or perceived to be real. And what's critical to understand here is that the victim's perception and whether the danger is real or not doesn't matter. What does matter is that fear can be psychological or physical and it can be rather incapacitating and debilitating. Making leaving the relationship quite impossible.

And I want to mention that the reason why I'm not mentioning gender here is because whilst women are the victims in the vast majority of cases. They are not in every single case and men can be and are still abused in some cases, so I don't want to put a gender here instead of the word *victim* and help to reinforce a damaging stereotype.

Additionally, to help show the importance of this topic some more, here are some numbers from the United States' National Coalition Against Domestic Violence. For example, 1 in 9 men and 1 in 4 women experience severe intimate partner physical violence, intimate partner contact, sexual violence, intimate partner stalking with impacts. These impacts include fearfulness, post-traumatic stress disorder, use of victim services, injury and more.

Furthermore, 1 in 3 women and 1 in 4 men have experienced some kind of physical violence in the past by an intimate partner. This includes a range of behaviour, like slapping, pushing and shoving, and in some cases might not be considered "domestic violence" when it actually is.

1 in 4 women and 1 in 7 men have been victims of severe physical violence. For example, beating, strangling and burning by an intimate partner in their lifetime. As well as 1 in 7 women and 1 in 25 men have been injured by an intimate partner.

Therefore, as you can clearly see (or hear) regardless of the situation (except maybe the last one) regardless of gender a sadly high number of both have experienced domestic violence. And this only highlights why it's critical to increase awareness of the topic.

What Is Coercive Control?

Moving onto the next section of the episode, one of the leading authorities on this area is a person called Dr Evan Stark and he defines Coercive Control as the following:

"a strategic course of oppressive behavior designed to secure and expand gender-based privilege by depriving women of their rights and liberties and establishing a regime of domination in personal life."

As well as one of the problems with the literature on Coercive Control is that there is no, or no easy to find studies that have men as the victims. Now it would be great to imagine that meant no men fall under this area, but given how the myth of men being domestically abused is false. I personally doubt this and think this is a massive gap in the literature. You cannot seriously imagine that out of every single man on the planet, not a single one of them is being Coercively Controlled.

Moreover, Stark adds in his work that 60% to 80% of all abused women experience Coercive Control beyond the use of physical abuse. Meaning the physical abuse might have stopped but the Coercive Control continues.

And Coercive Control can have deadly consequences as Stark argues Coercive Control is strongly correlated with murder. For example, for the sake of illustration only, between the years 2000 and 2006 3200 American soldiers were killed in combat, but during the same time three times as many women were murdered by their husbands or boyfriends. As well as 1 woman is murdered every 16 hours in the United State either by a current or former male partner.

With the victims most at risk of being murdered are the people in which domestic violence, stalking and Coercive Control happen at the same time. And domestic violence and stalking is common.

The Role of Narcissistic Personality Disorder:

Interesting, there is some evidence that Narcissistic Personality Disorder is involved in Coercive Control alongside antisocial personality disorder, as all three of them are common among perpetrators of domestic violence. With people having Narcissistic Personality Disorder being described as manipulative, demanding, arrogant and self-centred. And they exhibit at least 5 of the following traits:

- Exploitation of others
- A lack of empathy
- Envy of others
- Have a need for excessive admiration
- A grandiose sense of self-importance
- Busy with fantasies of unlimited power, beauty, ideal love, success and brilliance.
- A belief about themselves being special and can only be understood by or associated with special people and institutions.
- Arrogant, condescending attitudes or behaviours
- Sense of entitlement

How Is Coercive Control Criminalised?

Moving onto the last section of the episode, we need to address the very harsh topic of Coercive Control and the legal system. Due to very few elements of Coercive Control are technically a crime and criminal and psychological abuse is always harder to get evidence for and prosecute compared to physical abuse. And yes, I know physical abuse getting prosecuted is hard enough.

This sadly results in the identification, criminally charging and prosecution of the Coercive Control cases is very much beyond challenging.

To make matters worse, successfully prosecuting Coercive Control cases are incredibly rare.

Yet there is a bit of hope because if a case does move forward to trial then the case will most likely be plea-bargained.

In addition, if you live in Ireland, England, Wales, Scotland and France. Then you're in luck because those countries have criminalised Coercive Control but the United States does not. New York State has become the first state in the entire country to start introducing criminalising legalisation for Coercive Control as a class E felony. Which for myself and our non-US audience, it means that Coercive Control is punishable by a maximum fine of $250,000 dollars and/ or a maximum of 5 years imprisonment but more than 1 year.

And I just checked the New York State Senate Website for the bill and it says it is currently in committee. So it has another 4 stages to pass until it is signed or vetoed by the New York governor.

Conclusion:

At the end of this episode, I want to say that Coercive Control isn't just another facet of abuse to look at it. It is very serious that we need to address and I truly hope that none of you listening or reading this will ever experience it. And whilst we didn't look at how to avoid it and recognise the signs in this episode, I do want to do that in the future just to help protect all of us a little more.

But until then, Coercive Control and abuse might be a dark topic to look at. But it is fascinating and very much worth investigating, because you never know when it might be useful.

WHEN IS IT GASLIGHTING?

Concluding our look at recognising abuse and manipulation in relationships, we need to look at the scary, horrific and subtle form of abuse known as gaslighting.

Now, gaslighting is a very popular term in recent times and it is reasonably common to some extent, and it allowed victims and sufferers to name what was happening to them. But as the term started to gain popularity and currency, it started to lose its meaning. In this chapter, we look at what is gaslighting and most importantly, when is it gaslighting and when isn't it. This is a great chapter, you need to be aware of.

What is Gaslighting?

Gaslighting is a form of emotional abuse where someone uses psychological manipulations to cause another person to question their reality. It can happen between two people in any relationship. Like friendships, working relationships and romantic relationships. The gaslighter preserves their own sense of self and power over the other person who ends up adopting the gaslighter's version of reality over their own.

The reason why we need to look at this is because it's important to distinguish gaslighting from normal and healthy behaviours. Like disagreeing and we need to understand when a conflict turns into gaslighting.

When Is it Gaslighting?

Therefore, to understand this harmful behaviour, the easiest scenario to see when something is not gaslighting is something similar to this fictional one below.

Harry and his sister Claire used to spend a lot of time together and every Saturday you would go together, and bring your families along. Then when the pandemic struck they were forced to move their Saturdays together to a few hours on Teams together and they would catch up, play games and have dinner together.

However, when the pandemic eased and the restrictions were relaxed. Harry started going back out, going out on day trips and living life again to the fullest. Yet Claire wasn't comfortable with that and she doesn't feel like going out too much. So, the siblings spoke and they don't agree on where to go for their Saturdays together, because Harry wants to go out-out somewhere nice and Claire wants to stay in.

Resulting in the siblings being judgemental about each other, and each one is calling the other selfish, inconsiderable and horrible. As well as Claire might accuse Harry of not wanting to spend time with her and her family.

Now this isn't gaslighting because even though both siblings are interpreting the same facts very differently, and they want the other sibling to adopt their perspective. They aren't causing each other to question their own reality and they aren't trying to manipulate each other.

However, this could turn into gaslighting if one of the siblings were so insistent on their interpretation that it caused the other one to start doubting themselves. This would create a power imbalance in their relationship that would allow the gaslighter to undermine the victim's sense of self. As well as the gaslighter's need for control, the very act of manipulating and leveraging of power of this relationship are essential components in gaslighting.

And hurt feelings and challenging each other's viewpoints is not gaslighting.

On a personal note, I think it would be rather tragic if those things were gaslighting because it means you could never question other people or challenge their views on anything. I suppose that would also put clinical psychology in a difficult spot considering it's our job to challenge the client's maladaptive coping mechanisms, and cognitive processes.

As a result, if we apply this knowledge to our fictional example, if Claire was the sibling who was more powerful and pushed Harry around. Then Harry would be vulnerable to Claire gaslighting him in adulthood. Especially if Harry really does start to believe he is selfish, awful and horrible person by not submitting to Claire's wishes. Then he might start withdrawing from their relationship.

Again this would result in a gaslight dance if you will, because if Harry ends up being unable to sleep at night at night because he's wondering if Claire is right and he is selfish. Because he fears she's right about him not wanting to spend time with her then he's starting to question his own character and the very integrity of her relationships.

Then gaslighting is very much present.

<u>You Need Two People To Gaslight</u>

Moving onto the last section of the episode, I want to mention that gaslighting happens when there is a power dynamic within a relationship that ends up causing the person being gaslighted to question themselves, along with their sense of reality.

Typically, the gaslighter is constantly manipulating and attack the gaslightee as well as being verbally aggressive towards them.

In addition, the gaslighter is very likely to turn a discussion between the two into a blaming game against the other person. And they will most probably outright lie about what took place just to further their own manipulations because if the gaslighter is so certain about something then it's easy to make you question if you're memory or perception is right.

Then it all ends up leaving the victim of the gaslighting to feel worn out, unsure of themselves and wondering if they are crazy like the gaslighter said, and they might even end up avoiding future discussions out of fear of disagreements escalating this already disorienting discussion.

Additionally, the most concerning thing is that over time the victim may even accept the gaslighter's views of reality as their own. And these are critical defining elements of gaslighting.

However, the most critical to remember when it comes to gaslighting is that it can only work if there are two people taking part in it. The gaslighter and the victim. In other words, gaslighting can only happen if the victim allows it to.

You can keep yourself from ending up in a gaslighting relationship by being aware of the topic and the sort of language used in arguments. As well as how it makes you feel, and noticing how you react to it.

Some helpful phrases that might be helpful to stop you engaging in a verbal loop or power struggle include:

- "What you said hurt my feelings and I'm too upset at the moment to talk about it,"
- "Let's agree to disagree,"
- You're twisting what I said. Let's take a break and talk about it later,"

Conclusion

To wrap up this social psychology episode, I must admit that as more and more people use the word "gaslighting" in our world, we risk its meaning becoming blurred or forgotten. Therefore, it is critical that we clearly understand what it actually means and when something is and isn't gaslighting. Sometimes you will be involved in disagreements, it's natural, but sometimes you might meet person who wants to gaslight you.

And that's when you need to be aware of what's going on for your own sake, but just remember sometimes a disagreement is simply that. Two people disagreeing and not gaslighting in the slightest.

EXCITED FOR NEW THINGS, GOING TO LET BOUNDARIES DOWN (YOU'RE HUMAN) AND THINKING ABOUT ENDINGS: LESSONS LEARNT FROM SESSION NINE

This next session was definitely a mixture of positives and negatives, as is most of the therapeutic and healing journey. Thankfully, a lot of really positive things had happened in this past week and there were a lot of exciting things happening in the next few days.

For example, the day after this therapy appointment, I was going out and spending one-on-one time with a friend I made back in September. And that went really well actually, we spent four hours together, we spoke constantly and it was lovely that I was able to spend one-on-one time with them without me having a mental breakdown or mental health crisis afterwards.

We spoke about everything and nothing whilst we had lunch together, then they went off to a seminar at 5 til 6 in the evening. Personally, I still think that is a brutal time for a seminar but it meant we could spend a lot of time together, which was nice.

When it came to the counselling session, the day before I spent one-on-one time with this new friend, we focused on celebrating and acknowledging the fact that this was major progress. It was great that I was able to do this and I was looking forward to it.

Of course, I was nervous and anxious about spending time with this friend. My mental health had proven time and time again that this could end very badly, I could get seriously hurt and this could really decrease my mental health.

However, I wanted to do this for me, for my recovery and I wanted to try and prove to myself that I was ready. In reality, you probably shouldn't try to "prove" things to yourself because I have done that before it has been awful and my mental health has died because of it.

Thankfully, because I feel safe, because I have my therapy techniques and because I *know* I am safe with this friend, I was willing to try it. And thankfully, everything was fine and me realising that I am okay to try new things has really helped me, my mental health and my life because I have tried a lot of new things since this day and it has been great.

Another positive that I was excited about was I was no longer distressed and I didn't have PTSD reaction to the sound of kissing anymore. Since my best friend and Ruby could be kissing and being a couple in the same room as me and I didn't have to run out the room being distressed as hell.

I will admit that there has been one or two times when I have had to leave a room by casually walking away just to make sure that I was okay. I wasn't overly distressed but I needed in that moment to leave so my mental health didn't tip over.

This is a good reminder that us survivors are the most important people to ourselves and we need to do what we need for us. For example, I could have stayed in the room and there was a chance that my distress would build and build over time and I would have a mental health crisis. Yet I decided it was best for me to take a few minutes out, do some self-soothing techniques and then go back downstairs into where my best friend and Ruby were.

As a survivor, you are the most important person to you and you have to do what is best for you and your mental health in the moment. It is always best if you take a few minutes or an hour compared to staying in a situation that will trigger and distress you.

Please focus on yourself.

You are more important than you will ever know.

Personally, it felt really weird that I could sit in the same room as two people lightly kissing and not get triggered or reminded of my rape. And my counsellor mentioned it might be a good idea to decrease my use of the word "trigger" because I am not getting triggered as much anymore. Instead I am being reminded.

Being triggered means you have PTSD or trauma responses. For me, this means feeling like I was going to get raped again, I would feel terrified, I would feel physical sensations of him touching me again and so on.

However, at this moment in my recovery, I am actually not experiencing those responses. Instead, sure, the sound of kissing will remind me more often than not of what He did to me that night. That will never be okay but it is just a memory, just an event and just something that happened to me a few months ago.

I survived, I am healing and He can never touch me again.

In a moment, I'll mention a topic my counsellor was concerned about and we had a long conversation about it, because she didn't want me to get hurt again. Yet a final area that we celebrated was a day this week, I managed to sit in the gym café without being triggered or even reminded of my rape.

You might remember from a few chapters ago that I mentioned that the gym, sportswear and athletics in general was very triggering for me because I was raped in sportswear. Which being completely honest was a massive inconvenience because guys in sportswear are a major turn-on for me.

Therefore, my best friend was in the gym and I was up at the university anyway because I took them and I wanted to get some work done anyway, so I went to the library then sat in the gym café afterwards. I saw lots of guys and women in sportswear and I remember some of the guys looked hot and stunning.

Yet I wasn't triggered, I didn't feel scared and I didn't feel like my life was in danger. That was a massive sign of healing, progress and it was a little weird because this major, major trigger for me wasn't a trigger anymore.

That opened up a lot of great opportunities for me, because it means I can go to the gym, I can happily go to places where sportswear is a probable option and more.

I love healing and it just goes to show that healing is possible if you put in the work, have a good counsellor and in my experience, a very good workbook.

Spoke About Talking To A Guy

For context, the Saturday before my 8th counselling session I was feeling very lonely, I was struggling with my mental health and I was readjusting to the new reality that my best friend needed to take a step back as I spoke about in previous chapters. I felt like I didn't have any friends (even though I do) and I really wanted to make some extra friends.

So I did something that was a little dramatic when you take the context of my rape into account.

I've mentioned before that the context for my rape was I was sick and tired of never being allowed to be gay because I had been in fear for my life for so long during my adolescence and young adulthood. I simply wanted a hookup so I could have sex but it was a hookup that went wrong so he grabbed me, didn't ask my consent and so on. I've written about it in my other sexual violence psychology books.

Yet this hookup happened on the gay app, Grindr.

Therefore, this Saturday, I was feeling very lonely, my mental health was relatively good but not amazing so I downloaded the app with the sole aim of meeting people on it and finding friends. Of course, 99% of the people on this particular app only want sex, as a survivor that is not something I was after at that point. Even now maybe 4 or 5 weeks after this counselling session, I want to talk to people for a while before I even start thinking about having sex with someone.

I am still a virgin at the time of writing and I am okay with that. Virginity doesn't actually mean anything. You can read more about my thoughts on sexual violence and virginity in *I Am Not A Victim, I Am A Survivor.*

Anyway, between that Saturday and this ninth counselling session, I was talking to a particular guy and we spoke every day about a range of things. None of these things actually touched on sex. We mainly spoke about our degrees, where we were from, our thoughts on different topics like religions, philosophy (he studied them for his degree), games, movies and so on.

Given the context of my rape, my counsellor was concerned then I assured her that I was not looking for a relationship. In hindsight, maybe I was lying because I wouldn't mind a relationship with this guy but I was always going to pursue a friendship first and foremost.

Over the course of the session, me and counsellor spoke and I mentioned that my best friend recommended that me and this guy call first to see if we wanted a friendship and it removed the scariness (and possible dangers) of meeting a stranger one-on-one. This was before I went out with my friend the next day so we didn't know if I could handle a one-on-one situation.

My counsellor agreed this was a good idea

and then I mentioned that my best friend had stressed that they were going to tell me when I was allowed to meet this guy one-on-one. At first (as I mentioned to my counsellor) that I wasn't happy with this, because surely my best friend was taking my autonomy away from me. Then I realised my best friend has experienced in this area so I probably should listen to them.

My counsellor agreed with me that I should request a call when I was ready.

That was interesting and a feature in next week's counselling session for sure.

<u>You're Human So You Are Going To Let Your Boundaries Down</u>

This event focuses on the Wednesday before this session, so this happened on the same day as my eighth counselling session.

I've mentioned before that I'm transgender because I'm non-binary, so I go to a trans social group where I talk to my friends, hang out with people and just meet others like me. It's where I met my best friend amongst some of my other closest friends.

In addition, the 20th November every year is known as Transgender Remembrance Day to remember all the trans people that have been murdered all over the world in the past year. Sadly, the number of trans people being murdered is only increasing year-on-year and given the state of the world, this number will only increase in the coming years.

A lot more innocent people are going to be murdered for no reason. It's disgusting. This is why supporting trans people, survivors and other minority groups is so important.

Anyway, the trans group I go hold to a Trans Day of Remembrance service on the 20th November and they need people to read the names of the dead out for each month of the year. Therefore, the organiser of the group was struggling to find a final person to read out the month of December, so she asked me.

Now I am dyslexic (even though I wouldn't be officially diagnosed for another two weeks), I struggle with saying names and I did not want to do this. Yet she kept asking me, I kept saying no but then I gave in.

I wasn't happy but I was okay until I made the connection between consent, boundaries and fear. I was so scared that there were parallels between the organiser wearing me down, me not standing up for my own boundaries and reinforcing them and there were a lot of other rape parallels that I was struggling with.

I was scared for the future because if a lovely woman who I have known for maybe 16 months wore down my boundaries and I didn't reinforce them with someone I trusted. How the hell could I reinforce them with a stranger?

Was I a failure for not reinforcing boundaries? Was I failing in my counselling? Was I making a mistake that could play out in a different situation and get me raped again?

I was distressed as hell.

However, as my counsellor mentioned in the ninth session, we are all only human and we are going to lower our boundaries at times. It doesn't make us flawed, failures and it doesn't mean that we aren't recovering.

It just means that we are human.

Of course, we should always try to make, reinforce and challenge others when they cross our boundaries. Yet ultimately, if we let a boundary slip from time to time, then that is normal. Especially when it comes to our friends and loved ones.

Not reinforcing boundaries only becomes

a problem if you consistently let people walk over your boundaries.

Personally, this did help me feel better because since then I have reinforced other boundaries so I know this was just a slip. And that's okay because that is natural.

We need to be kind to ourselves and remember the self-compassionate steps I've mentioned before.

<u>Thinking Of Endings</u>

The charity that I get my specialist counselling from allows you to have up to 12 sessions of counselling with the possibility of more, but that isn't generally needed. Yet because I have been doing so well, my counsellor was wondering if I could finish early so I agreed to finish at week 11 instead of Week 12, because I wanted it, I didn't think I needed it anymore and I was happy to end it.

I had to make sure that I wanted to end it early for me instead of someone else's need. For example, I did have to think about whether I should end early so someone else could have my slot, but then my counsellor reminded me that I am just as important as the next person who fills my slot. I needed to make this decision for me.

After I realised I did want this to end early for me, my counsellor started to talk about what are endings like for me. Personally, endings are very abrupt for me. A lot of people just tend to abandon me, a lot of people and relationships just end without me knowing and there is never a sense of closure. For example, my childhood best friend was ripped away from me because of the lies and concerns of other people who didn't understand I was autistic and not a danger.

My nephews and nieces were ripped away because of my brother's girlfriend's toxic family stopping us from seeing them. that's actually happened twice now with two different girlfriends, so I have nieces and nephews that I was really close with but I no longer see. That's hard for me.

And there are countless other examples too.

Of course, I suspect a lot of this friendship and relationship stuff is because of my perception as outlined in the cognitive approach to mental health, but still. These endings were never nice.

As a result, my counsellor wanted to know what my idea of a good ending of the counselling would look like. This made me very excited as a clinical psychology student because I've heard a lot about how endings are critical in therapeutic work otherwise it can completely undo all the gains and success in a therapy.

I wasn't sure how I wanted this ending to look.

My counsellor explained that one client watched the last ever episode of Friends with her and they were both crying their eyes out. Another client wrote a poem and another one a story about how the counselling had impacted her, and another client had wanted coffee and cake. As well as one client had wanted a certificate so my counsellor had made that for her.

I still had no idea what I wanted for the ending of the therapy, but I have always liked coffee and cake. So I mentioned that was what I wanted for my final session in two weeks' time, then we could talk about anything and do paperwork in the final session.

She would bring the cake, and I asked for a coffee and walnut cake because I hadn't had one of them for years, and I was tasked with bringing the coffee.

It was going to be a wonderful way to end my counselling and that just gave me something else to look forward to in the future.

Something I never ever could have imagined nine weeks before.

FRIENDSHIPS, DISTRESS, TRAUMA: LESSONS LEARNT FROM SESSION 10

This had to be one of the most impactful and important counselling sessions and thankfully, it was the penultimate one. Since if you've been a long time reader of mine then you might be aware that friendships cause me a lot of distress. A lot of this comes from autism and my family refusing to get me diagnosed as a child as I could never access any support, people would think I was a creep and an idiot instead of an autistic person who didn't understand how the social world worked, and I have a lot of friendship trauma too.

I have been abandoned by a lot of friends over the years for different reasons, the majority of them not my fault and they happened because of the misunderstandings of other people (not actually my friends) so that led to people leaving and trying to ruin friendships etc.

That's a topic I've written about in other places.

Therefore, even now, I struggle with social relationships and I generally struggle with friendships. Both in terms of maintaining them by developing deeper, more meaningful friendships as well as developing them in the first place.

Now I am very grateful that in specialist counselling for sexual violence, you can talk about anything that brings you a lot of distress besides the sexual violence trauma. Making friends and being one-on-one was a major trigger and difficulty I had because of my sexual trauma, so this was connected.

The reason why I brought it up in this tenth session was because I asked for a phone call from the guy I had been talking too online, and that didn't go to plan so my autistic and traumatised mind went into overdrive. And my best friend made a cutting revelation about me that caused me a lot of distress for no reason.

Firstly, the Wednesday after my ninth counselling session, I texted the guy I had been talking to and I asked him something along the lines of, in the future would he be up for calling so we can see about being friends, meeting up in person and perhaps developing a relationship. Neither one of us had mentioned a relationship but I was curious.

He messaged back saying he wasn't sure what he wanted at the moment because he wasn't going on dates as much as he used to, he was focusing on his university presentations and assignments and he wasn't looking for anymore friends at the moment because he had enough and he didn't want to devalue anyone.

My traumatised mind went slightly panicked at this, because this wasn't how I intended this conversation to go. I did not understand how someone could talk to a person every day for at least nine or ten days and not be interested in a friendship, and I was seriously confused that people could have too many friends.

My trauma and my autism said that was impossible.

To make matters worse, we were talking on Snapchat which I have never used before. I screenshotted his message to send to my best friend because I had no idea how to respond. But the interesting thing about Snapchat is that it alerts the other person if you screenshot a message.

That created some tension and made me even more distressed because the other guy apologised he had hurt me, so I needed to explain what I'm bad at this friendship stuff, I didn't know what to say so I asked my best friend for advice and then later on I mentioned that I had a lot of trauma around relationships and that I was raped, so I was so new to this.

In other words, I was a wonderful chaotic mess.

He was very nice, kind and we spoke a little more that night over text but then I didn't talk to him for another week until after this counselling session. The only reason I started talking to him again was I do like him, I think he's cute and we both admitted that we like talking to the other because we had good conversations. And even though I doubt an in-person or an actual friendship would form, I would like to be friends in the future.

And he's just someone else to talk to and in the past few weeks, my mindset has changed. I do have a lot of good in-person friendships so having an online one isn't going to harm me.

In fact, I messaged him a few days ago and he replied to me earlier (normally he replies on the same day but it's near Christmas so everyone is busy) that I need to reply to.

That was the first part of my friendship distress in the week before this session.

The second part was I was very stressed, anxious and worried about meeting with my friend one-on-one the day after session eight. Since I did not want it to go wrong under any circumstances, but I did put a lot of pressure on myself which maybe I shouldn't have.

Instead it might have been a good idea if I had used my compassion steps and other self-soothing techniques. However, given what had happened with this guy the day before, how I was so distressed I couldn't calm down because I was working a Postgraduate Open Evening outside in the freezing cold so I couldn't use any self-soothing techniques. As well as an interview for a good additional role at my student ambassador work went wrong because there was an admin and communication error, I was severely distressed.

If those things had not happened the day before then I don't think I would have been so distressed about meeting up with a friend one-on-one (that wasn't with my best friend) for the first time since I was raped.

The final friendship-related distress was because my best friend made a very cutting revelation about me, and I do not believe that they meant this as a bad thing, or that it was something I needed to move heaven and earth to change. Yet I was so distressed, so anxious and my mental health around friendships was not the best that I took it as a major character flaw in myself.

My best friend mentioned how I only get to form friendships and want to get close to people that I am attracted to and want to get into a relationship with. Then they listed the five relationships that I have formed (and tried to form before the other people drifted away) since I was raped where that had been the case.

And this shouldn't be the case because this isn't healthy.

My traumatised mind went even more panicked about that because it was so true, and my best friend had been right about a lot of other things about my mental health and trauma so surely they were right about this too.

In reality, they weren't a hundred percent right and it is best if I don't take everything they say as truth even if it is right to some extent.

These three major stressors about friendships and social relationships really damaged my mental health for the next four days. My mental health was better for the counselling session but it seriously hadn't been for about half of the week.

My counsellor said that people who go through typical development without childhood trauma tend to go through certain stages of making friends. Around the ages of 13 to 16, teenagers make a lot of friends based on romantic and sexual attraction and they go through a lot of friends as they try to figure out what they like and don't like in people and potential partners. My counsellor explained this as remember how most teenagers have partners that last a week or a day at most and then they change it again with someone new.

Then around the age of 16, teenagers start to think beyond looks and physical attraction as well as they want something more permanent. As well as, this continues into adulthood moving away from physical attraction being the most important thing and they continue to develop their thoughts, feelings and emotions towards personality and psychological characteristics that they're attracted to.

However, when someone experiences childhood trauma, like I was in fear for my life because my social world was so homophobic so I thought if I made friends, got into a relationship amongst other things that I would be killed. This leads to stunted development so I was never able to do these stages that a typically developing child or teenager gets to do.

Therefore, my best friend was right in the sense that I do have a tendency to form friendships and want to become close with people I want to form relationships with. Yet they were wrong to say this wasn't entirely healthy or good, because developmentally I am still moving through the stages that other people go through.

And I am passing through the stages.

Because I am basically 10 years behind on this social development because it's only been recently that I am even remotely safe enough to start exploring who I am, who I like and what sort of people I am looking for. I'm still exploring the 13- and 16-year-old side of friendships.

Although, nowadays, I am starting to form relationships and friendships with people who might not be physically attractive but I think they're great people that I would really enjoy being in a relationship with because *they* are great people on the inside. For example, the friend I made back in September and I spent one-on-one time with them for the first time in this particular week. They are not my normal type but I like them because they're interesting, we both study psychology, we're both passionate about trans mental health research and we have other things in common too.

Another example is that I briefly had a friendship with a guy over the summer who I met during student ambassador work, and sure, he was physically attractive with his slim body, longish brown hair and boyish looks. Yet I was actually attracted to him because we could talk for hours upon hours about certain topics without getting bored and I liked *him* for him.

Therefore, it was so helpful for me to understand that I wasn't deeply flawed, I wasn't weird and I wasn't as toxic as people in my past had made me out to be. I am a traumatised person simply trying to recover and I am healing and recovering my life. This friendship forming is just part of the process.

In addition, as my counsellor said, David and Victoria Beckham, the main bond between them is physical attraction. For some people, physical attraction is important and the main driving force behind their relationships and friendships. It doesn't make them bad people, weird people or messed up.

Physical attraction just works for them.

So if physical attraction is my main driver in friendships and attraction then it doesn't matter, because it works for me and I do have deep and meaningful relationships in my life.

The main takeaway that my counsellor mentioned after the above was that I shouldn't accept everything my best friend says as truth. Yes, they've been a lot of trauma counselling themselves and they're had a lot of traumatised friends too. Yet they don't have a degree, they don't have any qualifications and they don't know the psychological theory and research behind everything.

Whereas the mental health professionals do.

Personally, even now about three weeks after this counselling therapy, I am not sure if I am angry or upset with my best friend about this. I suppose I am a little because they caused me so much distress because they thought they knew better about me and how I made friends (even though they were the exact same as me up until recently). So I am annoyed that they added to my distress for no reason.

Equally, I am sort of glad that they did mention it because it allowed me to learn about this development, that I am okay and I am making progress through these developmental stages. So maybe, all the distress was sort of worth it to some extent.

Quick Notes On Self-Soothing Techniques

As a result of me getting very distressed last Wednesday, my counsellor recommended that it would be a good idea if I made a list of self-soothing techniques that I could do in different situations so I could self-soothe even if I was very busy. Since I believed that I simply couldn't self-soothe because I was working Outreach then I was at a remembrance service so there was no time for me to focus on myself.

However, there are different self-soothing techniques I could do in different situations that help me better cope with being very distressed.

Therefore, if I was distressed when I was with other people, like my friends, besides from leaving the room and calming down that way. I could talk to my friends about what was troubling or distressing me, or I could talk to them about anything else, so this would get my mind to stop thinking about whatever's distressing me.

If I'm distressed and I'm home alone, then I can self-soothe by listening to music or one of the many podcast episodes that are always on my downloads. As well as I could do work on my laptop to help me relax, feel better and to get me to stop thinking about whatever's distressing me.

Me going on my laptop was a useful technique that I realised after talking to a woman on a rape support online chat before the servers crashed and the chat was ended. Just before the chat was terminated because of the technical issue, I realised that I was distressed because I kept ruminating about it so I needed to go on my laptop, do some things and that would help me not to focus on it as much.

Finally, when I'm busy and there isn't time for me to go on my laptop, talk to friends or do any of the other techniques that I mentioned in earlier chapters. Then I can do my breathing exercises to help me to calm down a little, I could play short songs through earphones (like I flat out love the Nezuko theme song from the anime Demonslayer), I could listen to short podcast episodes and I could imagine something relaxing and then make sure that I actually do it later on.

That could be a very powerful and useful technique that I need to try out when I get distressed again.

Overall, whenever it comes to distress and dealing with the negative emotions that trauma brings up, it is very useful to know at least a few self-soothing techniques that you can use in different situations.

An unofficial tip for you is after you read this chapter come up with your own list of self-soothing techniques that you can use in the following areas of your life:

- When you're with other people
- When you're with strangers
- When you're at work
- When you're home alone
- When you're outside alone

You might not believe you need this list of self-soothing techniques now but it is always better to have them and never need them, then need them because you're distressed and not have them.

Useful Quotes:

I wanted to end this chapter by mentioning two useful things that my counsellor said through the session. It was helpful because it helped me realise that I just need to let my emotions out, I need to allow myself to experience whatever my mind and body want me to experience, as well as experiencing these emotions are better than not. Keeping emotions bottled up is never a good idea.

"Let emotions flow and let it all come out,"

"There's nothing wrong in going to uncomfortable places,"

HOPE, HEALING AND EXCITEMENT: CONCLUSIONS FROM A FINAL COUNSELLING SESSION

There isn't a better way to wrap up this book that has been difficult, heartbreaking and distressing as hell to write at times than to finish off with a conclusion based on the final counselling session. I was partly surprised how great I felt, how excited I was for the future and how lovely the ending was.

It really was the perfect end to a great course of counselling that had allowed me to heal, thrive and get excited about the future. Not only because my PTSD, anxiety and other trauma responses were greatly reduced to the point where it doesn't cause me much distress.

Yet because it was a course of therapy that had changed my life forever and it had given me a lot of valuable skills that I can use with my own future clients too.

Therefore, as I start to wrap up this final chapter and conclude this great healing journey that I have been on for eight months now, I want to tell you what you can expect from a final session as well as all the great things that happened in that session.

The start of the session really highlighted how much progress that I've made over the past 11 weeks because there was nothing to actually report on or talk about. Sure, I had gotten distressed a few times by different things but I had my self-soothing techniques. I listened to my music so I didn't continue getting distressed, I went on my laptop to do some fun projects so I could disengage my brain and I talked to friends outside of my mental health.

I enjoyed talking to them and spending time with them, not because I needed mental health support but because they're my friends and I like them for them, and they like me for me. That was a very useful mindset shift that I had, because I can still lean on my friends from time to time but as my best friend said, I needed to support myself more.

And thankfully because of my rape counselling, that Healing Sexual Trauma workbook and my own research on the podcast that you have full access to over the course of these three sexual trauma books, I have all the skills I need to be able to cope on my own.

I can go back to having friendships because I love my friends, I enjoy hanging out with them and we have fun together.

That is a brilliant result to have after the past 11 weeks when my best friend was my lifeline, and we both made mistakes that led to us having an unhealthy relationship, and now I can feel closer to my other friends. I understand that I can be closer to people without us going through some mental health stuff together, and that people can care about me without being able to support me.

I know a lot of this might sound obvious to some people but as someone who's autistic and been raped, this was a very hard concept to understand.

Overall, I am really proud of myself that there was nothing to report, talk about or things that I needed advice for at the end of this session. That is major progress considering every single session for the past 10 weeks there has been something important or distressing I wanted to talk to her about.

Now I am back in control of my life, instead of my mental health controlling me.

Final Bits of Paperwork

Whenever you go for specialist counselling, you will need to complete a final set of paperwork so the mental health service can use it in their research, fundraising and reporting. For example, whilst we had our coffee and cake (more on that in a moment), we completed another set of CORE measurements so she could see how my distress had decreased and ability to function increased. Thankfully, I scored a 12 and anything below a 21 is deemed as clinically normal, so I was more than happy with that.

And interestingly, that is a massive decrease since the 7th session (the last time) I did the CORE measurements because I had scored around a 35 at that point and now I'm a 12. That's a great improvement.

Of course, you might not have such dramatic reductions in your symptoms, levels of distress and increases in your ability to function. That's okay.

We are all different people and it's okay if you're healing "better" or not as well as someone else. Healing is a journey and most of the time, progress will be immensely small, so small at times that you won't be able to notice it but you are in counselling, you are trying and you are using the skills and techniques that counselling teaches you in your own life.

You are making progress, and over time that progress will add up to something amazing.

In addition, I completed a form that I've completely forgotten about, and the final form was designed to be a part of the centre's fundraising statistics. You were given three answers out of "Improved", "Stayed The Same" and "deteriorated". Then the questions were along the lines of:

- Over the course of this counselling, my mental health has…
- Over the course of this counselling, my symptoms have….
- Over the course of this counselling, my ability to function has…

Those types of questions so the centre say in fundraising efforts something along the lines of "Give us money because 90% of survivors found our counselling improved their ability to function".

As you can see I do not work in a marketing department and I probably should never work in a fundraising department, but you get my point.

Personally, I'm more than happy to take part in this research and answer these questions, because I know it's important. As a researcher myself, I know how important data is so these sort of questionnaires can give mental health services invaluable insights into the effectiveness of their work.

In addition, I know how tight budgets are and how much pressure mental health services are under, so if there is any way that I can help them. Then I want to take it, not really for myself because filling in these forms has no real impact on me.

Yet I do it for you and all the other survivors.

I want to give the service data so they can campaign, receive money and so many other clients can receive the same, great support as I did.

And so other people's lives can change for the better too.

Overall, in the final session of your specialist counselling, you will have to do some paperwork. Not only so you can see how much progress you've made but to help the centre (which is probably a charity) so they can see their work is important and they can receive money to keep helping fellow survivors.

Coffee and Cake

There are two things I really love in this world besides writing, business and psychology. Okay maybe I love a lot of great things in this life, but I really love my coffee and exploring different types of food. Unfortunately, in the UK, it is very hard to find coffee cake anymore so when my specialist counsellor asked me what I wanted to do for my final session, I said coffee and cake.

A few of my friends have laughed at the idea because they were so surprised and it was so different from their mental health sessions, but they didn't experience sexual violence thankfully.

Therefore, I chose coffee and cake because to me that was the best way to end a series of counselling sessions about something as awful and evil as sexual violence. It's almost like the end of a good story, I had been fighting like hell for 8 months with my mental health, my PTSD and just struggling to stay alive.

However, after all the pain, all the agony and all the trauma that my idiot rapist unleashed on me, there I was. I was alive, happy and my mental health was so good I could happily sit down and eat cake without any fear, any worries and I could just talk to my counsellor like a close work colleague.

The ability to have something as normal as coffee and cake was a major achievement for me, because that was honestly the most normal thing I had done since I was raped.

And it felt amazing.

So after the paperwork as we sat there drinking our Nescafe coffee (yes I had brought seriously good coffee for the final session) and we ate the great cake that she had found, we talked, chatted and laughed about the state of mental health services.

She picked my brain about mental health services, what needed to improve, how bad the state of the UK's National Health Service was and how it needed to change in the future to be fit for the 21st century.

I was in my element as we debated and talked about my degree and this area of psychology that I am seriously passionate about, because this is why I want to work in clinical psychology. I want to help people, I want to transform lives and I want to help make the world a better place.

It might be a grand idea and hope, but even small actions can have a massive impact, so I am excited for the future.

I never would have said that 11 weeks ago.

Moreover, we discussed how she's learnt a lot from me over the past 11 weeks. She's started reading research papers again because she wants to learn, she wants to see what new methods are about and she is excited to learn again. That was only because of me, and that is a great thing to know.

Therefore, dear reader, when it comes to the end of your counselling or therapy for sexual violence, even if your therapist doesn't do this sort of thing, think about how you want to celebrate your journey.

You have done amazing because you are healing, you are alive and you have had to deal with more than most people have to deal with in their entire life, but you have survived.

It probably felt impossible, draining and like life could never ever get better but you survived and you went through therapy to start your healing journey. That is amazing progress so celebrate it.

Think about what *you* want to do to celebrate and mark this great event. The end of your therapy and end of the most intense part of your healing journey is a sensational achievement.

Celebrate it.

Some of the ideas that my counsellor gave me when I was talking to her included one client had watched the final ever episode of Friends with her. It was emotional and she was watching the end of an era on her final counselling session. It was poetically beautiful.

Another client had my counsellor make her a certificate, another client wanted to do drawings and yet another wrote a story about how therapy had impacted her and her emotions and she read it to my counsellor.

You can celebrate and mark the end of counselling however you want to. Whatever helps you mark this as an ending for you and will help you move on.

The Actual End

Ultimately, as we reach the end of this book, as I said to my counsellor, thank you for everything you have helped me to do and I wish you all the best for the future.

Without you, you wonderful reader, I couldn't have written this book, there wouldn't have been any motivation and there would have been no motivation for me to think of lessons to reflect on each week. You are the sole reason this book came into being and you have helped my healing more than you could ever know.

So thank you from the bottom of my heart.

And now that you've seen all my ups and downs, struggles and triumphs, you know that the healing journey isn't linear and there will be hardships ahead. Yet it is worth it, it is wonderful and it is one of the best things you can ever do for yourself.

So please, as we end this book, embark on your healing journey, find a professional who works with sexual violence survivors and start your journey towards healing and recovering from your trauma.

It is time to take back control of your life instead of your trauma controlling you.

You've already picked up this book so you must be interested in healing, and with that drive and determination and sheer willingness to start healing, I don't doubt you can heal fully.

Thank you for everything dear reader, and I wish you all the best with your future.

And I am proud of you for finishing this book and starting your healing journey.

REFERENCES

Linehan, M. M. (1993). Skills training manual for treating borderline personality disorder. Guilford press.

Linehan, M. M. (1993). Skills training manual for treating borderline personality disorder. Guilford press.

Almaliah-Rauscher, S., Ettinger, N., Levi-Belz, Y., & Gvion, Y. (2020). "Will you treat me? I'm suicidal!" The effect of patient gender, suicidal severity, and therapist characteristics on the therapist's likelihood to treat a hypothetical suicidal patient. Clinical Psychology & Psychotherapy, 27(3), 278-287.

Alshehri, T., Mook-Kanamori, D. O., de Mutsert, R., Penninx, B. W., Rosendaal, F. R., le Cessie, S., & Milaneschi, Y. (2023). The association between adiposity and atypical energy-related symptoms of depression: a role for metabolic dysregulations. *Brain, Behavior, and Immunity*, *108*, 197-203.

Aminoff, S. R., Onyeka, I. N., Ødegaard, M., Simonsen, C., Lagerberg, T. V., Andreassen, O. A., ... & Melle, I. (2022). Lifetime and point prevalence of psychotic symptoms in adults with bipolar disorders: a systematic review and meta-analysis. Psychological medicine, 1-13.

Blanchard, M., & Farber, B. A. (2020). "It

is never okay to talk about suicide": patients' reasons for concealing suicidal idealisation in psychotherapy. Psychotherapy Research, 30(1), 124-136.

Bower P., Byford S., Sibbald B. et al., Randomised controlled trial of non-directive counselling, cognitive-behavior therapy, and usual general practitioner care for patients with depression. II Cost Effectiveness. British Medical Journal. Dec 2000;321:1389.

Brockways, Laura Hale. 12/30/21. 59 Phrases to Help You Set Boundaries. PR Daily. https://www.prdaily.com/59-phrases-to-help-you-set-boundaries

Brown, S., Rodwin, A. H., & Munson, M. R. (2023). Multi-systemic trauma and regulation: Re-centering how to BE with clients. *Journal of Human Behavior in the Social Environment*, 1-18.

Chae, W. R., Baumert, J., Nübel, J., Brasanac, J., Gold, S. M., Hapke, U., & Otte, C. (2023). Associations between individual depressive symptoms and immunometabolic characteristics in major depression. *European Neuropsychopharmacology*, *71*, 25-40.

Choi, K. J., & Kangas, M. (2020). Impact of maternal betrayal trauma on parent and child well-being: Attachment style and emotion regulation as moderators. Psychological Trauma: Theory, Research, Practice, and Policy, 12(2), 121.

Coleman, J. (2024). Rules of Estrangement: Why Adult Children Cut Ties & How to Heal the Conflict. Random House.

Collins, K. A., Eng, G. K., Tural, Ü., Irvin, M. K., Iosifescu, D. V., & Stern, E. R. (2022). Affective and somatic symptom clusters in depression and their relationship to treatment outcomes in the STAR* D sample. *Journal of Affective Disorders*, *300*, 469-473.

Corrigan, F. M., Fisher, J. J., & Nutt, D. J. (2011). Autonomic dysregulation and the window of tolerance model of the effects of complex emotional trauma. *Journal of psychopharmacology*, *25*(1), 17-25.

Craparo, G. (2014). The role of dissociation, affect dysregulation, and developmental trauma in sexual addiction. *Clinical Neuropsychiatry*, *11*(2).

De Luna, J. E., & Wang, D. C. (2021). Child traumatic stress and the sacred: Neurobiologically informed interventions for therapists and parents. Religions, 12(3), 163.

Deaton, J. D., Wymer, B., & Carlson, R. G. (2021). Supervision strategies to facilitate vicarious post traumatic growth among trauma counselors. Journal of Counselor Preparation and Supervision, 14(4), 12.

Deutsch, R., Drozd, L., & Ajoku, C. (2020). Trauma-informed interventions in parent–child contact cases. Family Court Review, 58(2), 470-487.

Deutsch, R., Drozd, L., & Ajoku, C. (2020). Trauma-informed interventions in parent–child contact cases. *Family Court Review*, *58*(2), 470-487.

Dold, M., Bartova, L., Kautzky, A., Porcelli, S., Montgomery, S., Zohar, J., & Kasper, S. (2019). Psychotic features in patients with major depressive disorder: a report from the European group for the study of resistant depression. The Journal of clinical psychiatry, 80(1), 16309.

Dong, M., Lu, L., Zhang, L., Zhang, Q., Ungvari, G. S., Ng, C. H., ... & Xiang, Y. T. (2020). Prevalence of suicide attempts in bipolar disorder: a systematic review and meta-analysis of observational studies. Epidemiology and psychiatric sciences, 29, e63.

Dong, M., Zeng, L. N., Lu, L., Li, X. H., Ungvari, G. S., Ng, C. H., ... & Xiang, Y. T. (2019). Prevalence of suicide attempt in individuals with major depressive disorder: a meta-analysis of observational surveys. Psychological medicine, 49(10), 1691-1704.

Dubue, J. D., & Hanson, W. E. (2020). Psychologists' experiences conducting suicide risk assessments: A phenomenological study. Canadian Journal of Counselling and Psychotherapy, 54(4), 819-845.

Frankl, V. E. (1992). Man's search for meaning: An introduction to logotherapy (4th ed.) (I. Lasch, Trans.). Beacon Press

Friedrich, M. J. (2017). Depression is the leading cause of disability around the world. Jama, 317(15), 1517-1517.
Friedrich, M. J. (2017). Depression is the leading cause of disability around the world. Jama, 317(15), 1517-1517.
Gunter, E., Sevier-Guy, L. J., & Heffernan, A. (2023). Top tips for supporting patients with a history of psychological trauma. *British Dental Journal*, *234*(7), 490.

Guo, Z. P., Chen, L., Tang, L. R., Gao, Y., Qu, M., Wang, L., & Liu, C. H. (2025). The differential orbitofrontal activity and connectivity between atypical and typical major depressive disorder. *NeuroImage: Clinical*, *45*, 103717.

Harrison, L., & Wright, J. (2020). The experiences of person-centred counsellors working with suicidal clients online through the medium of text. British Journal of Guidance & Counselling, 48(4), 576-591.

Hazler, Richard J., Counseling and Psychotherapy Theories and Interventions. Chapter 7: Person-Centered Theory. 6th Ed. 2016. American Counseling Association.

Herman, J. L. (1998). Recovery from psychological trauma. *Psychiatry and Clinical Neurosciences*, *52*(S1), S98-S103.

Herman, J. L. (2015). *Trauma and recovery: The aftermath of violence--from domestic abuse to political terror*. Hachette uK.

Herman, J. L., & van der Kolk, B. A. (2020). *Treating complex traumatic stress disorders in adults: Scientific foundations and therapeutic models*. Guilford Publications.

Hershler, A. (2021). Window of tolerance. *Looking at trauma: A tool kit for clinicians*, *23*, 25-28.

https://www.health.nsw.gov.au/mentalhealth/psychosocial/strategies/Pages/communicating-response.aspx

https://www.livewellwithsharonmartin.com/boundaries-healing-childhood-trauma

https://www.psychologytoday.com/gb/blog/making-the-whole-beautiful/202205/what-is-the-window-of-tolerance-and-why-is-it-so-important

https://www.psychologytoday.com/gb/blog/the-crime-and-justice-doctor/202107/coercive-control-entrapped-fear

https://www.psychologytoday.com/us/blog/beyond-mental-health/202407/when-it-feels-impossible-to-get-out-of-bed

Jarero, I., & Artigas, L. (2016). Instruction for the Butterfly Hug Method.
Jarero, I., & Artigas, L. (2016). Instruction for the Butterfly Hug Method.
Jenkins, S. (2018). Increasing tolerance for calm in clients with complex trauma and dissociation. In *Equine-assisted mental health for*

healing trauma (pp. 44-53). Routledge.

Jubb, H. (2017). The effectiveness of self-soothing techniques for people with PTSD in secure units. Mental Health Practice, 20(5).

Jubb, H. (2017). The effectiveness of self-soothing techniques for people with PTSD in secure units. Mental Health Practice, 20(5).

Khalfa, S., BELLA, S. D., Roy, M., Peretz, I., & Lupien, S. J. (2003). Effects of relaxing music on salivary cortisol level after psychological stress. Annals of the New York Academy of Sciences, 999(1), 374-376.

Khalfa, S., BELLA, S. D., Roy, M., Peretz, I., & Lupien, S. J. (2003). Effects of relaxing music on salivary cortisol level after psychological stress. Annals of the New York Academy of Sciences, 999(1), 374-376.

Luby, R. R. (2024). Sexual violence: a trauma-informed approach for mental health nurses supporting survivors. *Mental Health Practice*, *27*(4).

McCormack, B., McCance, T., Bulley, C., Brown, D., McMillan, A., & Martin, S. (Eds.). (2021). *Fundamentals of person-centred healthcare practice*. John Wiley & Sons.

McCormack, B., McCance, T., Bulley, C., Brown, D., McMillan, A., & Martin, S. (Eds.). (2021). *Fundamentals of person-centred healthcare practice*. John Wiley & Sons.

Mearns, D., Thorne, B., Lambers, E., & Warner, M. (2000). *Person-centred therapy today: New frontiers in theory and practice*. Sage.

Mendelsohn, M., Herman, J. L., Schatzow, E., Coco, M., Kallivayalil, D., & Levitan, J. (2011). *The trauma recovery group: A guide for practitioners*. Guilford Press.

Mok, M. C., Schwannauer, M., & Chan, S. W. (2020). Soothe ourselves in times of need: A qualitative exploration of how the feeling of 'soothe'is understood and experienced in everyday life. Psychology and Psychotherapy: Theory, Research and Practice, 93(3), 587-620.

Mok, M. C., Schwannauer, M., & Chan, S. W. (2020). Soothe ourselves in times of need: A qualitative exploration of how the feeling of 'soothe'is understood and experienced in everyday life. Psychology and Psychotherapy: Theory, Research and Practice, 93(3), 587-620.

Monahan, M. F., Crowley, K. J., Arnkoff, D. B., Glass, C. R., & Jobes, D. A. (2020). Understanding therapists' work with suicidal patients: An examination of qualitative data. OMEGA-Journal of death and dying, 81(2), 330-346.

Podlogar, T., Poštuvan, V., De Leo, D., & Žvelc, G. (2020). The model of dynamic balance in therapists' experiences and views on working with suicidal clients: A qualitative study. Clinical Psychology & Psychotherapy, 27(6), 977-987.

Qi, B., MacDonald, K., Berlim, M. T., Fielding, A., Lis, E., Low, N., ... & Trakadis, Y. (2020). Balance problems, paralysis, and angina as clinical markers for severity in major depression. Frontiers in psychiatry, 11, 567394.

Renger, S. (2023). Therapists' views on the use of questions in person-centred therapy. *British Journal of Guidance & Counselling*, *51*(2), 238-250.

Rogers, C. (2000). Person-centred therapy. *Six key approaches to counselling and therapy*, *1*, 98-105.

Scupham, S., & Goss, S. P. (2020). Working with suicidal clients: Psychotherapists and allied professionals speak about their experiences. Counselling and Psychotherapy Research, 20(3), 525-534.

Siegel, D. J. (2010). *The Mindful Therapist: A Clinician's Guide to Mindsight and Neural Integration (Norton Series on Interpersonal Neurobiology).* WW Norton & Company.

Steffen, P. R., Bartlett, D., Channell, R. M., Jackman, K., Cressman, M., & Bills, J. (2021). Integrating breathing techniques into psychotherapy to improve HRV: which approach is best?. Frontiers in Psychology, 12, 624254.
Steffen, P. R., Bartlett, D., Channell, R. M., Jackman, K., Cressman, M., & Bills, J. (2021). Integrating breathing techniques into psychotherapy to improve HRV: which approach is best?. Frontiers in Psychology, 12, 624254.
Stern, R. (2018). *The gaslight effect: How to spot and survive the hidden manipulation others use to control your life*. Harmony.

Tudor, K., & Worrall, M. (2006). *Person-centred therapy: A clinical philosophy*. Routledge.

Vidal, J., & Soldevilla, J. M. (2023). Effect of compassion-focused therapy on self-criticism and self-soothing: A meta-analysis. British Journal of Clinical Psychology, 62(1), 70-81.
Vidal, J., & Soldevilla, J. M. (2023). Effect of compassion-focused therapy on self-criticism and self-soothing: A meta-analysis. British Journal of Clinical Psychology, 62(1), 70-81.
Vreijling, S. R., Fatt, C. R. C., Williams, L. M., Schatzberg, A. F., Usherwood, T., Nemeroff, C. B., ... & Lamers, F. (2024). Features of immunometabolic depression as predictors of antidepressant treatment outcomes: pooled analysis of four clinical trials. *The British Journal of Psychiatry, 224*(3), 89-97.

Whiteley, C. (2024) CBT For Anxiety: A Clinical Psychology Introduction To Cognitive Behavioural Therapy For Anxiety Disorders. CGD Publishing. England.

Whiteley, C. (2024) CBT For Depression: A Clinical Psychology Introduction To Cognitive Behavioural Therapy For Depression. CGD Publishing. England.

Wood, K. M. (2023). Setting Boundaries: 100 Ways to Protect Yourself, Strengthen Your Relationships, and Build the Life You Want... Starting Now!. Simon and Schuster.

World Health Organization. (2021). Guidance on community mental health services: promoting person-centred and rights-based approaches.

Wright, J. (2009). Self-Soothing—A recursive intrapsychic and relational process: The contribution of the Bowen theory to the process of self-soothing. Australian and New Zealand Journal of Family Therapy, 30(1), 29-41.
Wright, J. (2009). Self-Soothing—A recursive intrapsychic and relational process: The contribution of the Bowen theory to the process of self-soothing. Australian and New Zealand Journal of Family Therapy, 30(1), 29-41.
Zaleski, K. L., Johnson, D. K., & Klein, J. T. (2016). Grounding Judith Herman's trauma theory within interpersonal neuroscience and evidence-based practice modalities for trauma treatment. *Smith College Studies in Social Work, 86*(4), 377-393.

Sign Up Bonus

Keep up to date with exclusive deals on Connor Whiteley's Books, as well as the latest news about new releases and so much more!

Sign up to get a FREE psychology book boxset.

Sign Up Now!

https://www.subscribepage.com/psychologyboxset

Subscriptions:

Never miss an issue!

3 Month Subscription… $19.99

6 Month Subscription… $39.99

12 Month Subscription… $69.99

Subscribe Up Now!

https://payhip.com/b/eoQ85

www.ingramcontent.com/pod-product-compliance
Lightning Source LLC
LaVergne TN
LVHW082339200926
848481LV00012B/3394
* 9 7 8 1 9 1 8 5 9 9 6 1 9 *